# WORKPLACE INVESTIGATIONS

Techniques and Strategies for Investigators and Compliance Officers

**BY MERIC CRAIG BLOCH, ESQ., CCEP, PCI, CFE**

Copyright © 2013 by the Society of Corporate Compliance and Ethics.
All rights reserved. This book or parts thereof may not be reproduced in any
form without the express written permission of the publisher.

Printed in the United States of America.
18 17 16 15 14 13 12   1 2 3 4 5 6 7

ISBN: 978-0-9792210-8-8

The views expressed in this book are those of the author. They do not necessarily
represent the views of his employer or any third party.

This publication is designed to provide accurate and authoritative information
in regard to the subject matter covered. It is sold with the understanding that
neither the authors nor the publisher are engaged in rendering legal, accounting, or other professional service. If legal advice or other expert assistance is
required, the services of a competent professional person should be sought (from
a Declaration of Principles jointly adopted by a Committee of the American Bar
Association and a Committee of Publishers).

*To order copies of this publication, please contact:*

*Society of Corporate Compliance & Ethics*
*6500 Barrie Road, Suite 250, Minneapolis, MN 55435*
PHONE *+1 952 933 4977* | FAX *+1 952 988 0146*
*www.coporatecompliance.org*
*service@corporatecompliance.org*

**To Jacob**
*It's important to keep your promises.*

# CONTENTS

**INTRODUCTION** .................................................................. 1

**PART I:** Getting Started ........................................................... 3
  A  The Workplace Investigations Process ......................................... 4
  B  Structuring the Process ...................................................... 8
  C  Understanding the Investigations Manager's Roles ............................ 13
  D  Establishing Internal Corporate Notifications ............................... 18
  E  Identifying Business Goals of an Investigation .............................. 20
  F  Setting the Timing of the Investigation ..................................... 22
  G  Selecting the Right Investigator ............................................ 23
  H  Selecting Investigation Team Members ........................................ 26
  I  Understanding the Rights and Responsibilities of Participants ............... 30

**PART II:** Conducting the Workplace Investigation ................................ 45
  A  The Four Critical Steps ..................................................... 45
  B  Understanding the Initial Report ............................................ 46
  C  Inquiry or Investigation? ................................................... 53
  D  Planning the Investigation .................................................. 58
  E  Investigator Best Practices ................................................. 62
  F  The Personal Interview ...................................................... 65
  G  Telephone Interviews ........................................................ 84
  H  Interviewing the Implicated Employee ........................................ 86
  I  Detecting Insincerity ....................................................... 90
  J  Common Interview Problems ................................................... 94
  K  The Interview Memo .......................................................... 99
  L  Collection and Review of Documents ......................................... 101
  M  Evidence Standards ......................................................... 103
  N  Reaching a Conclusion ...................................................... 110
  O  The Final Report ........................................................... 113
  P  Executive Summaries ........................................................ 123
  Q  Business Ethics Bulletins .................................................. 123
  R  Reporting to the Reporter .................................................. 125

**PART III:** Other Investigation Issues . . . . . . . . . . . . . . . . . . . . . . . . . . . . . . . . . . . . . . . . 127
   A  Special Concerns of Investigations . . . . . . . . . . . . . . . . . . . . . . . . . . . . . . . . . . . 127
   B  Protecting the Findings from Disclosure . . . . . . . . . . . . . . . . . . . . . . . . . . . . . . . 136
   C  Referrals to Law Enforcement . . . . . . . . . . . . . . . . . . . . . . . . . . . . . . . . . . . . . . . 141

**APPENDICES:** Conducting the Workplace Investigation
   A  Selling the Value of Workplace Investigations to Management . . . . . . . . . . . . . . . . 149
   B  Compliance & Ethics Issue Reporting and Response Policy . . . . . . . . . . . . . . . . . . 155
   C  Sample Mission Statement . . . . . . . . . . . . . . . . . . . . . . . . . . . . . . . . . . . . . . . . . 169
   D  Notification Matrix for Key Internal Departments . . . . . . . . . . . . . . . . . . . . . . . . . 171
       Glossary . . . . . . . . . . . . . . . . . . . . . . . . . . . . . . . . . . . . . . . . . . . . . . . . . . . . . 174
   E  Notification of Investigation for other Key Internal Departments . . . . . . . . . . . . . . 181
   F  Colleague Referral Guidelines . . . . . . . . . . . . . . . . . . . . . . . . . . . . . . . . . . . . . . . 183
   G  Guidelines for Outside Counsel . . . . . . . . . . . . . . . . . . . . . . . . . . . . . . . . . . . . . 189
   H  Management Notification of Investigation . . . . . . . . . . . . . . . . . . . . . . . . . . . . . . 195
   I  Request for Interview . . . . . . . . . . . . . . . . . . . . . . . . . . . . . . . . . . . . . . . . . . . . 197
   J  Request for Subject Interview . . . . . . . . . . . . . . . . . . . . . . . . . . . . . . . . . . . . . . 199
   K  Instructions to Witnesses . . . . . . . . . . . . . . . . . . . . . . . . . . . . . . . . . . . . . . . . . . 201
   L  Personal Statement . . . . . . . . . . . . . . . . . . . . . . . . . . . . . . . . . . . . . . . . . . . . . . 203
   M  Final Investigation Report . . . . . . . . . . . . . . . . . . . . . . . . . . . . . . . . . . . . . . . . . 205
   N  No Retaliation Memorandum . . . . . . . . . . . . . . . . . . . . . . . . . . . . . . . . . . . . . . . 207
   O  Business Ethics Bulletin . . . . . . . . . . . . . . . . . . . . . . . . . . . . . . . . . . . . . . . . . . . 209
   P  Close-out with Reporter . . . . . . . . . . . . . . . . . . . . . . . . . . . . . . . . . . . . . . . . . . . 211

**SOURCES** . . . . . . . . . . . . . . . . . . . . . . . . . . . . . . . . . . . . . . . . . . . . . . . . . . . . . . . . . 213

# INTRODUCTION

I am surprised that more people have not already written a book like this. The compliance industry is relatively new—compared to other staff functions in companies—but there are not many resources on how to conduct a relevant, business-oriented investigation. The handful of investigation books out there seem to focus either on traditional Human Resources investigations—I have always called them the "I hate my boss" cases—or are written by lawyers who handle existential-crisis investigations with allegations that threaten to destroy their corporate clients. But what about the other 80 percent of the problems facing professionals who are responsible for investigations: the kind that include personnel-management problems, operations deficiencies, management issues, and customer disputes?

I am also surprised that the compliance industry has not yet sufficiently addressed the role workplace investigations play in a company's ethics and compliance function. To me, investigations are the flip-side of codes of conduct, corporate policies, hotlines and training. Those are the proactive steps a company properly takes to establish its operating rules concerning these important issues. But those steps are essentially mechanisms to implement the rules of proper conduct. They are not ends in themselves.

Investigations are the reactive side of the coin. If a company's training, code of conduct and hotline leads an employee to report a concern of possible co-worker misconduct, is the compliance function now complete? Not in terms of helping the company. The company is helped when that report is investigated, areas for process improvement and unacceptable business risk are identified, the appropriate people are held accountable, and the results are reported upward. The compliance process is then complete.

So why hasn't the compliance industry placed greater emphasis on investigations training and maximizing the value of workplace investigations? I don't know. I am a frequent speaker on investigations at industry conferences. My sessions are filled with compliance professionals who are looking for practical guidance. Not just on how to conduct an investigation effectively, but also how to navigate the turf battles internally and convince their bosses to give them sufficient resources. The philosophical compliance messages, by themselves, do not seem to be enough. Their bosses also seem trapped in the stereotypes of "compliance people only seek an ethical paradise" and "an investigation is not needed because we can just fire Bob today." When I share my own war stories during the presentation and offer observations on these topics, I see nodding heads and welcome-to-my-world smiles that tell me that I am not alone.

This book gives you practical guidance from someone who is also in the trenches. I will leave the ethics, high moral principles, quick selling points, and philosophy to others. Instead, I want you to become a proficient workplace investigator. I want you to be able to add value to your company and its compliance efforts. I want you to be part of a process with integrity, trust and internal allies. I also want you to protect yourself personally and professionally from the risks that come with being an investigator of allegations that can get someone fired or possibly thrown in jail.

This book is intended both for investigators as well as compliance people who rely on others to conduct the investigation and report their findings. Those in the latter category need this book because the effectiveness of their function depends on the quality of the investigations on which they rely. Without some knowledge of their own, their success has been blindly mortgaged to the competence of someone else.

For convenience, this book uses the masculine form of pronouns although, of course, women can be investigators, reporters, witnesses, and subjects of investigations. Also, references to a "company" or corporate setting may be equally applied to any organization.

Meric Craig Bloch
*Livingston, New Jersey*

# PART I
## Getting Started

For some companies, the strategic planning around the workplace investigations process is preparing for the day when the company receives a catastrophic misconduct allegation, such as the apocryphal whistleblower reporting that the CFO has been shredding financial documents. Otherwise, not enough thought is given to its role in the company's operations. This shows both a poor allocation of company resources and a lack of imagination. If a critical incident occurs, the company's response will take on a life of its own regardless of how much advance thinking tried to plan for it. If the situation happens a second time, the company may not survive, regardless of how the investigation is managed.

The truth is that employee misconduct is usually of a lower magnitude. It arises in the ordinary course of business. It is comparatively minor and foreseeable from a personnel-management perspective. But employee misconduct, especially when repeated elsewhere in the company, quietly bleeds the company dry one drop at a time.

The success of the workplace investigations process depends, in great part, on the role and profile of the compliance program in your company. The challenge for resources comes from the fact that compliance programs are not profit centers. And like other cost centers, there must be some legitimate business purpose for funding the program. If your company funds the compliance program simply out of fear of prosecution or because your competitors have these programs, the future of the workplace investigations process is precarious. Created in that context, the group's continued existence within the company depends on factors outside its control. Similarly, if the program exists without concrete expectations and metrics to measure its business value, the group is also at risk because its value depends on the perceptions of business leaders that will necessarily change over time.

> **Process Pointer:** Devote some thought to the improbable goal of putting yourself out of business in your company. It will never happen, but it is a worthy goal. If you have such ideas as goals, it is more likely that you will get closer to that goal than if you do not.

Compliance officers and investigators must, if for no reason other than self-preservation, remember their obligation to contribute to the equity value of the business—increasing the returns to its shareholding owners—and this must be a fundamental operating principle. But remembering is not enough. Your executive management is going to have to be persuaded and periodically reminded that you are not just another layer of bureaucracy to be endured.

> **Process Pointer:** Investigators and compliance officers need to demonstrate their value to the company constantly. They need to understand how business executives think. A discussion of the management mindset and ways to highlight your value may be found in Appendix A.

## A) The Workplace Investigations Process

An examination of the workplace investigations process begins by answering some fundamental questions.

### *What Do We Mean by an "Investigation?"*

An investigation is the systematic and thorough examination into something and the recording of that examination in a report. In the workplace, an investigation has four components:
- Thoroughly documenting incidents of actual or suspected misconduct in order to maintain a permanent record of their occurrence.
- Identifying the root cause of an incident where improper conduct is suspected.

- Identifying people involved in misconduct.
- Compiling information that proves or disproves an allegation or that implicates or exonerates someone suspected of misconduct. This is especially true if the investigation is used to justify disciplinary or similar post-investigation action.

## *Who are the Customers of an Investigation?*

It is useful to use the term "customer" in referring to those who are part of your investigations process. Some employees may voluntarily seek your assistance, such as colleagues in Human Resources or executive management, to investigate a specific allegation. These people want help with a specific problem and seek a specialist to help them accomplish something. A "customer" is the executive manager who relies on the investigation's findings to improve business processes. A "customer" also includes someone who is involuntarily part of the process, such as an implicated employee, reluctant witness, or a manager who would prefer to wish the reported problem away.

## *What is the Purpose of an Investigation?*

A workplace investigation should seek sufficient credible facts to allow managers to decide what action, if any, should be taken in response to substantiated allegations. Responsive action may be divided into three broad categories:

- **Corrective Action.** Corrective action includes those steps taken to "fix the system" to minimize the likelihood of future wrongdoing or other undesirable events. Examples of corrective action include establishing, changing, or augmenting procedures; training; and implementing internal controls. Inspections or audits may be used to identify effective ways to address problems identified during investigations. Managers may decide to take corrective action even when the allegations cannot be substantiated but where a deficiency in internal controls is identified.
- **Remedial Action.** In some cases, the investigation reveals that wrongdoing or deficiencies in internal controls adversely affected the reporter or others. Although redress of wrongs is not, by itself, a sufficient reason to initiate a workplace investigation when other remedies are available, basic fairness requires that individuals

harmed by improper conduct or unintended consequences of "the system" be restored to their prior circumstances whenever possible. This action is an important element of management's response to a workplace investigation. Management may decide to take remedial action even when allegations of wrongdoing cannot be substantiated.

- **Disciplinary Action.** Disciplinary action is any action short of criminal prosecution taken against a person found to have engaged in wrongdoing. Disciplinary action does not include training, counseling, or performance-based actions. Disciplinary action, however, includes such actions as: admonition, reprimand, suspension, demotion, corrective action, written warning, or termination of employment. Although some may think disciplinary action by management is the primary purpose of a workplace investigation, corrective and remedial action is actually more relevant to the business goals of the company. In some cases, other considerations may dictate that no (or limited) disciplinary action should be taken in response to substantiated misconduct. (For example, to protect the integrity of the workplace investigations process, it may be necessary to forego disciplinary action in an unusual case to protect the identity of a reporter or other confidential source.)

## *What Matters are Appropriate for a Workplace Investigation?*

An investigation looks into matters that have some relationship to effectiveness, efficiency, integrity, ethics, and public confidence in the company. Therefore, allegations that improper conduct has adversely affected the business effectiveness of a company department are proper for workplace investigations. Because your company should recognize that improper conduct is likely to adversely affect one or more of these areas, it should be policy that all non-frivolous allegations of improper conduct are thoroughly and impartially investigated and reported. Most of these allegations will be investigated internally. However, as discussed below, some allegations should be referred to others for investigation.

Workplace investigations focus on allegations of employee misconduct. The difference among companies often depends on how the company defines "misconduct." If your company has a detailed code of conduct—and if the investigations function is linked to ethics training—then workplace investigations will follow the scope of the code of conduct.

Most codes of conduct are substantively identical. Specifically, misconduct falls within one of these specific categories:
- Accounting Irregularities
- Antitrust and other Competitive Issues
- Conflicts of Interest
- Confidential Information
- Employment Practices
- Fraud
- Insider Trading and Information
- Internal Business Operations
- Internal Workplace Conduct
- International Trade Controls
- Kickbacks and Bribery
- Misuse of Internal Company Systems
- Money Laundering
- Political Activities
- Records Retention
- Regulatory Noncompliance
- Retaliation against Whistleblowers
- Substance Abuse

The need for an investigation, however, does not arise simply because it is believed that your code of conduct was violated. Stated differently, the business value of the workplace investigations process should be more than just as an adjunct to the ethics process. The investigations function could be expanded to cover any of these issues:
- Deliberate or reckless attempts to circumvent normal business procedures or controls;
- Violations of Sarbanes-Oxley or any other law or regulation concerning corporate governance and oversight;
- Systemic or pervasive concerted action directed toward a group of people;
- Any involvement by a corporate officer or a member of the board of directors;
- Potential material financial impact to a business group or the company;

- Likely potential harm to the company's reputation or a risk of adverse publicity; or
- Likely potential for a significant lawsuit against the company.

***What Matters are not Appropriate for a Workplace Investigation?***
Certain allegations are not appropriate for a workplace investigation. Those types of allegations include:
- When certain allegations have been reported to the appropriate government authorities, such as major criminal activity and securities-law violations;
- Review of management business decisions, where there is no allegation of misconduct; or
- An individual's belief, without more, that he or she has been "wronged" by the "system." Company investigators are neither ombudsmen nor are they a substitute for management's dispute-resolution mechanisms, and they should not be used for that purpose unless there is evidence those systems are nonresponsive. Complaints from people seeking relief from adverse personnel or disciplinary actions, unfavorable findings in discrimination cases, or other matters for which a statute or regulation sets forth a resolution process, should be accepted for workplace investigation only when coupled with a non-frivolous allegation that management is unable or unwilling to address the matter fairly and impartially for reasons related to conflicts of interest or personal impropriety, such as retaliation for whistleblowing, or cooperating with an investigation.

## B) Structuring the Process

To ensure both functional effectiveness and a proper use of company resources, the investigative function should be tailored to your company's specific needs, depending on your company's history, industry, and key business risks.

### *Tailoring the Process*
There is no "one size fits all" workplace investigations process. You need a process that your leaders believe will best prevent, detect and explain

violations within the organization. Several factors will determine the contours of the process:

- Size of the organization. How formal and elaborate a process depends on the size, complexity and culture of your company. The industry in which your company competes should also be considered.
- The likelihood that certain types of misconduct may occur because of the nature of the company's business. When there is a substantial risk that certain types of violations may occur, management must develop a process that meaningfully detects and prevents those types of offenses.
- The company's history. This factor considers the types of offenses the company—or those of its competitors—should have taken steps to prevent in the past. Preventing the recurrence of known problems should be foremost in the minds of executives trying to make the investigations process effective and relevant to the company.

> **Process Pointer:** Some companies establish or restructure their investigations process to respond to a particular corporate scandal the company just survived. While past history should guide you, do not rely on it exclusively as your function's reason to exist. The process should not simply react to a specific event, and it should be sufficiently forward-looking to have a strategic purpose for the company's future. This will ensure the long-term viability of the workplace investigations function.

## *Funding the Process*

The principal resources of an investigations function are people, information, physical assets and financial assets. The determination of the primary focus of the function dictates how the function is structured and how resources are allocated. The amount of resources the company is willing to dedicate to the function determines how many investigators can be hired, what technology and equipment can be acquired, and even how high a corporate profile can be maintained.

Investigation funding is challenging because needs may be difficult to project and the investigation process is a reactive one (depending on the volume and type of reports received). One complex investigation, especially if it requires the engagement of outside experts, can skew the budget projection—or overrun—for a particular year.

One of the best ways to help fund the process adequately is to show the value contributed to the company or demonstrate that the process pays for itself. You may strengthen your budget justifications with any of the following:

- Focusing investigative goals on the company's strategic and business needs;
- Tracking historical investigations costs accurately;
- Implementing cost-effective strategies;
- Pursuing restitution and recovery where possible; or
- Quantitative estimation of risk avoidance.

### *Formal Corporate Policy*

If your company does not already have one, you need something from your company's board of directors or executive management to give you the necessary corporate authority to establish your process. The policy document serves as a statement from your company's leadership that the company affirmatively mandates the investigative process and that primary responsibility for this function is placed with you. A sample corporate policy may be found in Appendix B.

The statement gives the workplace investigations process credibility and authority in the company. A good policy also addresses functional needs. The policy should make your group responsible for the reporting to the company leadership of all misconduct-related matters. Even if fact-finding is handled by other departments in certain cases, all upward reporting should be done through your group.

Employees should be obligated to report matters of suspected or actual misconduct as part of their job responsibilities. Some companies give employees a number of places to report the incident, and others direct the employee to their whistleblower line. (The use of the whistleblower line is valuable when an employee wants to report misconduct but wishes to remain anonymous or feels uncomfortable using his own management chain.) There should be some internal mandate to speak up, or the workplace investigations process may not be able to detect something that might be going on because people didn't want to get involved or believed that nothing would be done.

Your group must conduct the investigations of any non-routine matters. (A non-routine matter is something that is not suspected to arise in the ordinary course of business.) Key internal departments like Human Resources should continue to handle the garden-variety personnel management matters they usually do.

Your group should be empowered to specify both the investigations process for the company and the investigation protocol to be followed. This will create the investigative benchmark for the company. Deviations from the standard are permissible as a particular investigation requires, but these articulated standards at least ensure that the deviation was the result of an informed decision and not inertia, indifference or bureaucratic turf.

The policy should specify periodic upward reporting obligations. There should be reports submitted monthly or quarterly so your company's leadership can assess the company's ethical health and areas of unacceptable business risk. (It will also let you continually showcase the value of the workplace investigations process to the company.)

The corporate policy should specify the basic structure of the workplace investigations function. But regardless of its precise contours, there are still certain considerations common to any company's investigation process, which the policy should address:

- What misconduct will trigger an internal investigation?
- To whom should the incident or misconduct be reported?
- When should an investigation begin?
- Who should conduct the investigation and how should it be conducted?
- What should be the purposes of the investigation?
- What types of disclosures outside of the workplace investigations process are necessary?
- What are the obligations of employees to report concerns, cooperate with investigations, not interfere with the investigation process, and be truthful when providing information to investigators?

> **Process Pointer:** If you can't get a board-of-directors mandate, why bother having a robust process? You then care more about the risks to the business than they do. You cannot survive without the board as your advocates.

You may also want to create your own Mission Statement to define—and clarify—the workplace investigations function's specific role in your company. A sample may be found in Appendix C.

## *Independence*

An investigation cannot even appear to be influenced by management. The independence of the investigations process ensures that the results are a fair determination of the facts learned. The company should consider placing the responsibility in an independent department outside the regular management structure, such as an independent compliance department. Interference for any reason, whether regarding timing, methods, witness selection, determination of documents to scrutinize or ultimate determinations reached destroys the credibility of the investigation process. The process will be viewed as an inquisition, a management tool, or just irrelevant to the business. It will also increase the risk of liability to the company.

## *Consistency*

Responses to allegations must be procedurally consistent and predictable. Employees must believe that the response to a report of actual or suspected misconduct will be handled the same regardless of the implicated person's management level.

## *Navigating the Political Winds*

A workplace investigation occurs within a matrix of competing business interests. Inside the company, the boards of directors, the audit committee, management, employees and shareholders often have different goals and perceptions of their interest. Players do not always put the company's interests above their own personal or professional goals. Outside the company, competitors, the press, the company's auditors, the market, and the government all have varying motives and concerns.

One of the most important things you can do is convince upper management—and the board of directors if necessary—of the importance of understanding and solving the problem under investigation. This is crucial to obtaining adequate resources and authority for the investigation and to obtain proper credit for helping the company deal with the problem.

## C) Understanding the Investigations Manager's Roles

Traditionally, investigations were conducted by members of the legal or human resources department. There is now a trend toward more autonomy, professionalism and objectivity in the management of this process. There are some clear advantages for the use of an independent workplace Investigations Manager to oversee the investigation process. Accordingly, the investigations manager could be your Compliance Officer or someone in that department who specializes in investigations.

### *The Corporate Counselor*

The Investigations Manager supervises the overall investigations process and the workplace investigations process. The manager is responsible for keeping the process working and the investigation objectives in focus.

The Investigations Manager has more than just a procedural role. The manager must have the skills to translate the value of the investigation process and findings into forms of risk management and business counseling. The manager must have nontraditional compliance competencies such as business partnership, industry knowledge, communications skills and teaching. Business expertise and financial skills enhance the manager's value further.

Because investigating possible misconduct and its related business failures involve questioning someone's judgment and putting a stop to activities that may be both popular and lucrative, the Investigations Manager needs sufficient tact and clout to carry out the function. Similarly, because company policies will be investigated, the manager should have experience both in the company generally and as a manager to be credible to those who may be investigated or to whom the findings are reported.

However, some will claim that the appointment of an Investigations Manager undermines the goal of encouraging corporate colleagues to work together amicably by threatening the cohesion that binds them. This view is correct only if investigations are conducted poorly. A properly conducted investigation—which includes an appreciation for your company's political forces at work—reassures management that the investigated deficiencies or errors are viewed in a realistic, marketplace context rather than a perfect world. The fact that the Investigations Manager must continue to work with these people, cultivate them as allies and customers of the investigative process, and encourage them to refer future matters actually makes it more likely that the Investigations Manager will be able to navigate internal operating forces successfully.

The investigative process is not an exact science. So the Investigations Manager must be sufficiently experienced and creative to represent the interests of the workplace investigations process to executive management. This requires good skills in "corporate diplomacy," especially when important executives would prefer a quick disposition to a matter that, in the best interests of your company, requires a more thorough examination.

The Investigations Manager needs to be more than an able defender of the process. The manager must also be open to an informal and open exchange of ideas with colleagues in other departments. Some investigations may need to be tailored—again, in the best interests of the company—to minimize disruptions to operations or to accommodate some unrelated business need. The Investigations Manager has to find some way to bring together the sum total of these competing interests and still ensure a proper investigative result.

### *The Process Controller*

An Investigations Manager specializes in investigations and should have significantly more experience than either the company's in-house attorneys or the human resources managers. These other professionals often, however experienced in their own disciplines, normally handle investigations as only a part of their traditional responsibilities. The investigations they conduct are also likely to suffer from their competing time priorities. Having a full-time Investigations Manager also shows that your company does not have a "part-time" approach to investigating workplace misconduct.

The Investigations Manager acts as the final authority and the solely responsible individual for the conduct of the investigation. The Investigations Manager must believe that the results of each investigation support the conclusions as to the type of the management decisions that are available, that are supported by the findings, and that can bring the matter to a conclusion.

A good Investigations Manager also understands the nature of litigation because that's where many investigations lead. The manager understands the concepts of evidence, discovery and the other issues related to litigation. As an employee, the Investigations Manager understands the workplace and business operations better than an outside counsel retained to conduct the investigation. The manager also understands the company's culture and the internal company politics that may expedite, or impede, corrective action. The effective Investigations Manager uses his or her knowledge of the workplace to help draw out the facts of the case. The manager will be better known to company management and its employees. This may result in more effective persuasion of company management that action is necessary and better cooperation in requests for information and interviews.

### *Case Management*

Case management means the internal procedures for collecting, recording, organizing and preserving all the various pieces of information gathered in an investigation. This is your company's official record of the matter. If there is a lawsuit, regulatory action or prosecution, these are the key materials that will be reviewed to determine if your company's actions were proper or if your company may pursue a claim affirmatively.

Case management is necessary in all types of investigation. Proper management begins when the report is first received. It continues until the investigation is closed and the findings are reported.

The Investigations Manager is singularly responsible for case management. This includes each of the following duties:
- Ensuring that proper notes are taken, whether of interviews or physical examinations;
- Preparing, or causing the preparation of, official reports that document the investigator's activities; and
- Maintaining separate case folders for each investigation that contain all the reports, documents, and other information relating to the investigation.

Case management keeps track of what has been done and what needs to be done in an investigation. Proper documentation and updating allows all interested parties to understand the basis for any later company action. If the investigation extends over a long period of time, proper case management allows the investigator to refresh his or her memory and to identify any facts that remain to be developed.

## *Using Technology in Case Management*

Most companies use computer software to track investigations and develop analytics of investigative trends. If your company chooses a technology platform for case management, the Investigations Manager should be responsible for maintaining the investigations database.

A case management platform allows for easy case assignment and workload management. It facilitates the need to monitor progress of an investigation, assign specific tasks and keep investigators from becoming overloaded. Specifically, a good platform allows the Investigations Manager to ensure each of these:

- Document each report received of actual or possible misconduct;
- Confirm that appropriate authorizations are in place and internal notifications have been made to begin the investigation;
- The progress of each investigation is timely and adequately reported;
- Financial issues such as asset values and estimated losses are recorded;
- Investigation objectives are tracked and updated;
- Case resources are managed;
- Post-investigation information is recorded.

## *The Investigations Manager as Trainer*

Teaching investigative skills (especially to part-time investigators in other departments) and specifying your company's investigations protocol are vital responsibilities of the Investigations Manager. Training should be conducted in a variety of ways to suit the existing skills and experience levels of the investigators. A good way to train investigators, for example, is to assign the novice to work with a more-experienced investigator. Like many disciplines, classroom instruction in workplace investigations is only of limited value. It must be combined with controlled, practical experience to be a valuable learning tool.

The Investigations Manager establishes guidelines in advance to avoid allegations that the company proceeded on an inconsistent or capricious basis. Taking this step will minimize the time and effort spent addressing procedural issues when the need for an investigation becomes apparent. The guidelines should cover when an investigation will be conducted and how the investigation will proceed. The guidelines may also cover who determines the need for an investigation and who will oversee it. Specific guidelines also ensure the integrity and confidentiality of an investigation.

### *The Coach to the Investigators*

The Investigations Manager must also be the motivating force to the investigators. To them, the Investigations Manager is the face of upper management. The manager is their advocate and protector when the going gets rough. This is not a trivial point. There are a number of issues that investigators face, and each of these affect their attitudes and ability to close a successful investigation:

- Being required to defend your findings in court, to regulators and second-guessing executive management;
- Spending extensive time and effort on an investigation that is later shown to be based on false allegations, reports or information;
- Investigations may not be resolved, terminated without resolution or may result in what the investigator believes is an inappropriate disposition;
- Some investigations may stretch out for an extended period, leaving investigators to feel that they are not making sufficient progress;
- Investigators may be subject to ethical temptations;
- Witnesses and corporate colleagues may be uncooperative or frustrating;
- Executive management may not share the investigators' sense of urgency or decide that an identified problem is not as serious as they do.
- The reluctance of law enforcement officials or prosecutors to accept a case after significant effort has been expended;
- Investigators may become cynical and pessimistic about the integrity of their colleagues.

An Investigations Manager is not required to be a psychologist to be effective. However, being alert to these signs will ensure an efficient and effective workplace investigations process.

> **Process Pointer:** Think of the Investigations Manager as part quarterback, traffic cop and big brother to the process. And to senior management, the Investigations Manager should be seen as equal parts "reality therapist" and "organizational pathologist."

## D) Establishing Internal Corporate Notifications

If the workplace investigations process is going to be useful to your company, you must ensure that you learn of incidents when they arise. The need is most clearly identified with incident management. For example, some companies have a plan specifying roles and responsibilities once executive management learns of a serious incident that threatens the company. This presents the second hurdle to overcome. Incident-management plans are often generic documents admonishing employees to report a list of actual or suspected incidents to their superiors when they occur. This "silo" approach may accomplish the upward reporting of incidents, but such a plan does not ensure cross-department notification of incidents.

At the other end of the spectrum, it isn't much better. Don't just rely on your hotline. Most of those calls are of the "I hate my boss" variety. Referrals from other key internal departments are your best sources for matters to investigate. A model matrix may be found in Appendix D. A template memorandum to notify other key internal departments that you received a report whose subject matter affects their part of the business may be found in Appendix E.

The notification matrix has a simple goal: the notification to and inclusion of key internal departments in the resolution of a specific incident category. The matrix does not determine which department leads the resolution of the problem, but it ensures that each department with a stake in its resolution will be included. (In reality, because each incident will have unique facts and varying internal concerns, it is not helpful to define responsibilities in advance. Proper discussion internally will often divide responsibilities easily.) Including these internal departments facilitates the resolution by making that department's substantive skills available to the investigation.

The first step in preparing the matrix is to define those categories of risk your company faces. Your company's code of conduct is a good first step. Then the company should also identify (i) what level of risk exposure requires immediate action; (ii) what level of risk requires a formal response strategy to mitigate the potentially material impact; and (iii) what events have occurred in the past, and at what level were they managed?

Your goal should be a workable document that can be reasonably understood throughout the company. Use plain English and common-sense definitions. Don't worry about including every factual variation of an incident that falls within the category. Be extra careful if the matrix will be distributed internationally and used by non-native English speakers.

Don't forget that company bookshelves are filled with formalistic "thou shalt" policies. Coupled with the fact that most employees want to do the right thing but are not always sure what the right thing is, there is no reason not to craft a matrix that gives practical guidance. It is a meaningless exercise if it will not be accepted and integrated into your company's operations.

The second step is to identify your company's key internal departments. For most companies, the legal, human resources and finance departments are obvious choices. Be sure to include specific business groups because they are a key reporting source of incidents. This will also create some loyalty with those groups because most incidents will affect the revenue stream from an impacted customer, and the matrix provides for their involvement. Consider, if appropriate for your company, other departments such as corporate security, internal audit, or public relations.

The third step, of course, is to determine which departments will be notified for a specific incident category. The compliance office should always be notified. Once the assignments are done, executive management should formally approve the matrix and agree to abide by it.

Early knowledge about misconduct-related incidents often eludes compliance departments, especially in larger companies. Do not discount the fact that the matrix will also assist the necessary efforts that ensure effective reporting to the group of actual or suspected misconduct. Adhering to the matrix, therefore, enhances the quality and quantity of the information you will collect and report to executive management.

Because the goal is to actually learn of incidents, do not just rely on the matrix. Give practical instructions to the people who usually inform you. These practical instructions can be basic referral guidelines to let them know about what, when and how to inform you. These guidelines should mirror the basic structure of the matrix because it is a continuation of the same process. Sample guidelines may be found in Appendix F.

Mitigating the risks of foreseeable incidents with an effective investigative process should be critical for any company. It takes a concerted and ongoing effort to integrate the workplace investigations function with the functions of other internal departments to make an effective incident management program. Properly done, you have one more opportunity to demonstrate the value of their groups and to establish them further within the company's operations.

> **Process Pointer:** A good notification process is essential to the survival of your process. Otherwise, how can you have any confidence that you will be informed when incidents occur? And even with the process, don't forget your diplomacy and salesmanship skills to cultivate these key internal colleagues.

## E) Identifying Business Goals of an Investigation

The investigations process has its own business objectives. An understanding of these purposes helps establish the workplace investigations process in your company. Investigators are no different than any other company employee; your job is to serve a business purpose designed to protect and enhance shareholder value.

### Business-Focused Objectives

No investigation of any complexity can be successful unless specific objectives are determined in advance. The objectives of the investigation decide the investigation's starting point and where it is intended to finish. The objectives determine the fact-finder's purpose, measure the progress, and provide the framework by which the Investigations Manager builds the case for post-investigation handling.

Properly articulated objectives actually protect the company. They lay a defensive foundation against possible claims later on that the investigation was improperly motivated, a "witch hunt" or a rambling inquisition against imagined wrongdoing with no beginning or end. The company is protected when it can be demonstrated that, from the beginning, the intentions and objectives of the investigation were legitimate, professional and proper.

## *Determining the Facts*

Many companies treat the fact-gathering process to investigate a misconduct allegation as just a personnel-management matter. There is often little focus on professional fact-gathering methods, which can help to assure the credibility of the evidence. In the absence of a professional process, one that can be examined to determine the equity of the process and outcomes, the accuracy of the fact-gathering, other than as a way to justify terminating employment, remains a shortcoming in many companies.

The context in which your investigation is conducted must be to answer two basic questions: what happened and why. The investigative process determines the facts that are sufficient to cause a reasonable person to recognize that the true facts are what they are reported to be.

In a misconduct investigation, the accusations must be credible, relevant and truthful to bring the level of proof to a standard where management should be expected to determine responsibility. The investigation also determines whether any other people were involved besides the implicated person. By identifying the subject's modus operandi if misconduct is proven, you will identify gaps in internal controls.

## *Establishing Accountability*

An investigation establishes accountability as to how an event happened and what mitigating circumstances may exist that affected the outcome of the event. The investigation does not critique management style, unless specific management actions contributed to the circumstances which permitted the event being investigated to occur.

## *Maximizing the Decision Process*

Investigators are in the business of information gathering. Information developed from an investigation maximizes options for those managers who must decide on the solution. The only way management decision-makers can be offered the maximum number of options is if the investigation is done right.

## F) Setting the Timing of the Investigation

Investigations vary in complexity and the length of time to complete them. All investigations should be conducted as promptly as reasonably possible. A timely investigation gives the company more time to develop appropriate responses or defenses.

Timeliness is part of a professional investigation. Timeliness is important for other reasons as well:

- Innocent people should be cleared as soon as possible.
- Corrective action is generally more effective when taken closer to the triggering event.
- Ongoing misconduct must be stopped as quickly as possible.
- Morale may suffer in the investigated department while waiting for the outcome.
- Delays create the perception that these reports are not important.
- Over time, it becomes more difficult to obtain accurate statements (and some employees may leave the company).
- The investigation will assist in any legal action that may arise in connection with underlying matters.
- Promptness may be a mitigating factor in almost every level of government enforcement, and delay or indifference can be seen as an aggravating factor.

Whether a particular investigation is timely depends, of course, on the circumstances of that investigation. You should generally set a timetable that gives a reasonable amount of time to conduct the investigation. You must ensure the investigation's timely completion.

That being said, no investigation should be completed too quickly if that means that the quality of the resolution will suffer. You may have to resist pressure from outside sources—pressure that may be reasonable or otherwise—to either rush or stall a case. As with many things, balancing competing interests is the key.

## G) Selecting the Right Investigator

Choosing the wrong people to conduct an investigation will likely ensure a poor result. But the right investigator depends on the particular facts of the case. No person can proficiently conduct every type of investigation. The right investigators understand the business and the techniques needed for fact finding regarding that case's type of allegation. In addition, they will have credibility with the executive management and be seen as impartial with no vested interest in the outcome of their investigation.

You are the fact-finder. In some cases, you simply make the findings. In other cases, you may be the fact-finder, business counselor and/or dispute resolver.

A challenge in assembling the investigation team is the need to develop in the team an investigative mentality. An effective workplace investigations team shares some important qualities.

### *Relevance*

This quality is listed first because it is probably the most important. All the other qualities are immaterial if the investigation is not made relevant to the needs of the business.

Every risk is essentially a business risk. As an issue moves up the corporate structure, it becomes a business risk. A legal risk becomes a business risk at some point. A flaw in operations, a financial fraud, the misconduct of an important manager all become business risks.

This means that whatever the facts are that prompted the investigation, the investigation's output must be directed to how the business can benefit from the findings.

On a practical level, proper considerations of relevance will also ensure an efficient investigation because it keeps the investigation's scope limited only to the necessary issues.

### *Proper Mindset*

Doubt is a necessary quality for any investigator. You should remain appropriately skeptical. Do not assume that management or employees are honest and telling the whole truth until the facts are gathered and the inquiries are complete. Have sufficient imagination to develop sufficient theories against which to compare factual evidence as it develops. Persevere until the anomalies are resolved and the fact pattern is thoroughly understood. Finally, have patience to find the smallest detail that less-experienced people may overlook but that can provide that vital clue or inconsistency. You will discover the truth as a result of your ability to inquire and learn from that inquiry.

### *Professionalism*

The essence of professionalism is that you conduct the investigation with integrity, fairness and diligence. How the investigation is conducted reflects the professionalism of the company. The integrity of an investigation may often depend on the reputation of the investigator. You must be sufficiently senior to communicate and/or implement investigation plans. You must also be able to maintain the confidentiality of sensitive information.

Similarly, you must be fair and even-handed. If the employees believe that a rigorous investigation process applies to lower-level workers but somehow exempts the senior managers, the workplace investigations process will not survive.

### *Independence*

You must be free from actual or apparent bias or conflict of interest. Consideration must be given to whether an investigator's judgment may be affected or criticized by previous biases or political considerations, whether real or not. For example, an investigator should not investigate the conduct of his or her superiors. Also, investigators who witnessed the underlying conduct cannot participate in the investigation because they have independent knowledge of the events and may be a witness.

Independence means that everyone gets a fair chance, and that each implicated person is investigated in the same manner, with the same professional, impartial, objective treatment.

### *Competence*

The quality of an investigation also depends on your competence. You must have the skills that are matched to the type and nature of the investigation you are handling.

The ability to investigate and interview effectively are acquired skills. You must have the experience and the expertise to conduct a credible investigation. You must understand how to interview witnesses, manage documents and other records, and to maintain any applicable privileges to the extent possible. You should also be fully informed about company policies, procedures and company culture. You must know the management controls and strategies employed by the relevant business group. You must be able to contribute to the discussion of risks to the business, highlighting the potential likelihood or severity of risk areas.

Competence also includes the quality of accuracy. You must be able to effectively collect and sort data from a variety of sources, human and otherwise. You must be qualified and able to observe and accurately record data. The findings will depend on these skills.

## *Objectivity*

Throughout our lives, we develop a set of values. These values influence the way we live and the decisions we make. These values are subjective. They are shaped in part by gender, by education, by race, by intellectual capacity, and by personal experience. But these have nothing to do with the reported conduct in an investigation, which must be viewed objectively. Information must be reviewed and analyzed using the same standards, and the findings in an investigation should be based on the facts, not an opinion filtered through your personal value system. Understand and factor in your own natural biases.

You can demonstrate your objectivity in two effective ways. First, you can decide not to participate in determining the investigation's objectives. This might show that you had no particular interest in its outcome and, similarly, no personal agenda to pursue. Second, you can exclude yourself from the decision-making process at the end of the investigation. By not being party to the decisions regarding corrective action, such as employee discipline, you have no part in the outcome. Because you have no interest in the investigation's objectives and outcome, it might be difficult to accuse you of bias or prejudice in your findings.

> **Process Pointer:** Doubt does not equal cynicism or an assumption that everyone is lying. Doubt means that you refuse to assume things are true without proof and you always keep your mind open for other explanations.

Objectivity, however, does not mean jumping to conclusions without first independently corroborating the facts. The goal should be to allow the facts developed through the investigation to speak for themselves.

Project an air of objectivity. This can be done by choosing your words carefully during interviews and avoiding body language that might project an inappropriate attitude.

### *Fairness*

Fairness is important, but the term means different things to different people. Fairness to the people under investigation identifies you as a true professional.

Fairness means being truthful to witnesses. When an implicated person asks what proof exists against him, fairness means telling him the truth. It is not exaggerating the quality or quantity of the proof. It is not telling him that everyone thinks he is guilty when, in fact, only you believe that. Being fair sometimes means simply that you are being honest. It is being professional with both actions and words.

### *Thoroughness*

A good investigator follows all relevant leads to their logical conclusion and seeks to corroborate key findings. This means checking all leads and double-checking others. Some leads may appear to be of secondary importance, and you must make decisions regularly to strike the balance between efficiency and thoroughness. Pressures like time and resource constraints as well as the disruptive effects of investigations should be balanced against the need for a thorough examination of the facts.

## H) Selecting Investigation Team Members

The Investigations Manager determines the appropriate investigator for a specific investigation. If necessary, the manager should work in conjunction with internal audit, human resources or risk management if an investigation requires their assistance. The manager also retains private investigators, outside counsel, and certified fraud examiners as needed. Staffing the investigation requires a consideration of the advantages and risks of appointing certain personnel as investigators.

## Lawyers as Investigators

Lawyers are generally thought to be best-suited to investigate because investigations typically involve interviews with employees (some of whom may be hostile), the analysis of complex facts, and a final determination as to whether there have been any civil or criminal violations. Most lawyers are experienced at examining witnesses, sifting through facts, and ranking both in order of their importance. Certainly, experienced attorneys are able to determine the necessary obligations of the company in each particular circumstance, and counsel will make recommendations concerning what actions to take as a result of the investigation.

However, lawyers do not always make the best investigators. Although they are skilled in gathering evidence and preparing a case, their expertise is generally limited to some area of the law. Also, many lawyers never met a legal issue they didn't like. They can leave no stone unturned in analyzing an issue while losing sight of the big picture—the client's overall business needs.

Lawyers also may not have the skills needed to advise the company on whether and how to conduct its business operations differently in the future. Lawyers may be predisposed towards assessing risk rather than proposing a business-focused resolution. It would be unusual that they could serve in the other roles: as a business counselor, trouble shooter and operations improver. Learning about "bad facts" in an investigation is a tool to be used to improve the business, not a risk to be avoided lest the company get sued by someone who finds out about it.

There are also certain risks with using lawyers as investigators. An attorney who is directly involved in interviewing witnesses or gathering evidence may be a fact witness in a later suit, and thus may be disqualified from acting as the employer's attorney.

There are differences among lawyers, of course. Civil litigators can be useful but they don't necessarily make the best investigators as they sometimes tend to be predisposed to seek a certain result. A former prosecutor's investigative instincts may be preferable so long as the individual doesn't act too much like a prosecutor.

There may be a preference to having investigations conducted by your company's in-house counsel. The counsel's familiarity with the company, its policies, personnel and compliance politics is an advantage to the corporation. Investigations conducted by in-house counsel may be less costly and more efficient than one conducted by outside counsel. Employees may also be more willing to talk openly with in-house counsel than an outsider.

However, there exists the risk of perceived bias because your in-house counsel may be seen as a management representative, especially if a member of executive management or human resources is the subject. They may consequently appear less credible and independent. Credibility is essential to gaining the confidence of investors and regulators when there is a suspicion of wrongdoing.

Outside counsel will sometimes be retained for the investigation to provide a quick response and to fill the need for additional resources. These lawyers can also help where the existing compliance staff and the company's internal lawyers do not have the subject-matter skills needed for the investigation. Whenever it is essential to demonstrate that the fact finding was done by objective parties, it may be wiser to choose outside counsel.

Even if outside counsel is retained for your investigation, the investigation process should still be tailored to the same purposes as the in-house investigation. A sample guidance memorandum for outside counsel may be found in Appendix G.

### *Auditors and Accountants*

If the investigation requires reviewing financial records and an understanding of business processes, using auditors and accountants seems obvious. Auditors can be used to review documentary evidence, evaluate tips or complaints, schedule losses, and provide assistance in technical areas of the company's operations. Auditors are the ones who frequently detect the financial anomalies. They can also identify fraud indicators.

Accountants, however, generally have limited investigation experience. Auditors and their accounting counterparts also may not be able to complete an investigation that requires more than straightforward "number crunching" or fraud that lies beneath what appears to be proper financial processes and documentation. If the scope of the investigation includes a larger perspective on the operative facts—especially if witnesses must be interviewed—these professionals are better used in collaboration with other investigators.

## *Corporate Security*

Depending on the company, security department investigators are often assigned the field-work part of the investigation, including interviewing outside witnesses and obtaining public records and other documents from third parties. The drawbacks are that they often have little experience in workplace investigations and may have a limited view of the issues. Considering their day-to-day role, they may also attract unnecessary attention to the investigation.

Many companies hire former law-enforcement officers to work in their corporate security departments. This may appear sensible on one level. However, do not confuse the experience of someone enforcing public laws with that of investigating employee wrongdoing (especially when you are looking to identify areas of unacceptable business risk). There is actually little crossover between the two areas, and the skills of one area may not effectively translate to the other.

## *Human Resources Personnel*

The Human Resources department should be consulted to ensure that the laws governing the rights of employees in the workplace are not violated. Human Resources personnel can also be useful if the claims involve allegations of discrimination or retaliation. Their involvement will lessen the possibility of a wrongful discharge suit or other civil claim.

However, remember that these colleagues may have limited expertise in the relevant legal areas. Also, their investigative skills and abilities may be circumscribed because of the nature of their regular duties. Just because they have experience in human resources does not make them experienced fact-finders.

---

**Process Pointer:** Resist the temptation to use any investigator. For best results, match their skills to the type of investigation you are conducting. Experience in human resources or law enforcement does not necessarily make someone an experienced workplace investigator.

---

*Outsourcing the Investigation*

For a workplace investigations process, outsourcing may mean either the complete referral of an investigation to a third party, such as a law firm, or contracting out for selected or specialized investigative support services as needed. The decision to outsource is usually based on a cost-benefit analysis and the objectives of the investigation.

Outsourcing for specialized and expert services is almost always an important part of the budget and the approach to the workplace investigations process. The following are specialized services that are commonly used to support corporate investigations:

- Computer forensics
- Forensic auditing and accounting
- Handwriting analysis
- Document examination
- Surveillance
- Laboratory services
- Audio or video enhancement.

## l) Understanding the Rights and Responsibilities of Participants

The participants in a workplace investigation may be divided into the following categories: responsible managers; internal departments; reporters; witnesses; implicated people; suspects; and investigators. The participants likely have different perceptions of the purpose, scope or nature of a workplace investigation. Their respective rights and responsibilities also differ. These rights and responsibilities may impact the manner in which the investigation is conducted, its results, or the action that may be taken in response to the investigation.

*Responsible Managers*

Responsible managers are those who have management authority to take corrective, remedial, or disciplinary action in response to the findings of a workplace investigation. In practical terms, responsible managers are the superiors above the management level of the implicated person. Consequently, they are among the people for whom the investigation is to be performed, whether or not they initiated the request for the investigation.

When a responsible manager did not request the investigation, as, for example, when there is a hotline report, the responsible manager should be notified promptly upon commencement of an investigation, unless there is good cause to believe the investigation would be compromised by doing so. When compromise is a concern, consider whether a more senior person should instead act as the responsible manager.

Because responsible managers must take appropriate corrective, remedial, or disciplinary action, the investigation should provide them sufficient information to make intelligent decisions about these matters. In longer, more complex investigations, responsible managers may be provided periodic progress briefings. Their participation in decisions about the direction of the investigation may be encouraged if this will help ensure they obtain information necessary to make their decisions. Such participation may also help them understand the investigation is intended to promote the efficiency of your organization.

### *Internal Departments*

Internal departments are those business units in which the matter under investigation is alleged to have occurred. The implicated person's department should be appropriately notified of the existence and general nature of the workplace investigation. Premature notice that would compromise the investigation should be avoided. However, as a practical matter, the implicated person's department should be notified before the conduct of on-site interviews in most cases.

Notifying the implicated person's department at the earliest practical time is important because the managers have an affirmative responsibility to cooperate with and help facilitate the investigation. The managers' cooperation is often essential if the investigation is to be successful. Cooperation entails more than simply providing a space for the investigators to work and making witnesses available at reasonable times. It requires the managers to establish the proper atmosphere for the conduct of the investigation and, at times, positive assistance.

Depending on your needs and specific requests, this may include such actions as:

- Making a general announcement regarding the existence of the investigation in order to limit speculation and inform department employees of their duty to cooperate with investigators;

- Directing uncooperative witnesses to answer questions, and disciplining those who continue to refuse to cooperate;
- Taking effective action to prevent or address concerns about retaliation for cooperating with the investigation;
- Directing employees within the department to assist the investigation by gathering documents or other materials, conducting analyses of information, and adjusting meeting, vacation and travel schedules to be available when needed during the investigation.

Cooperation necessarily requires the implicated person's department not take any action that could be construed as interference with the investigation. Therefore, employees should not:
- Suggest what witnesses should say when interviewed or attempt to influence potential witnesses in any other manner;
- Question witnesses as to the nature of you questions or their responses;
- Take any retaliation action against reporters or witnesses; or
- Identify the reporter (whether anonymous or not).

You should not assume that department personnel will know intuitively it is improper to question witnesses about their statements, even in a casual manner. Therefore, these matters should be discussed when the implicated person's department is notified of the investigation.

## *Reporters*

Reporters are the people who present the initial information triggering a decision to conduct a workplace investigation. Reporters have many different reasons for making allegations, but their motive is not directly pertinent to your investigation. The allegations of a reporter who is seeking to "get even" may lead to the discovery of substantial misconduct. Some reporters choose to remain anonymous. Others may identify themselves but request confidentiality during the investigation. Other reporters have no objection to the disclosure of their identities during the course of an investigation.

When reporters have first-hand knowledge of facts related to the allegation, they should be interviewed as witnesses. Reporters who admit their own wrongful involvement in a matter they present for investigation, or who are implicated during the course of the investigation, may also become implicated people. Because bias may color the perception and recollection of any witness, investigators may find it useful to explore the reporter's motive in order to decide what weight to attach to facts asserted by the reporter, just as they would for any other witness. However, you must exercise caution to avoid leaving reporters with the impression they are being investigated or harassed for making the report.

Because reporters voluntarily present information concerning wrongdoing, there is a heavy burden on the company, in general, and you in particular, to ensure reporters are not subject to retaliation. Accordingly, a reporter's requests for confidentiality merit special consideration that may impact the conduct of the investigation and the potential for disciplinary action. You may find it necessary to interview reporters more than once because not interviewing them in their office at the same time co-workers are interviewed would appear odd and suggest they were the reporter. In some cases, you should attempt to develop alternate sources of evidence in order to protect the identity of reporters who have requested confidentiality.

Reporters should be told whether an investigation of their report will be conducted; doing so may reduce the likelihood they will request duplicative investigations from other organizations or take actions outside your organization. Reports may also be told when an investigation has been concluded. However, due to the implicated person's privacy rights, reporters do not have the right to know what specific remedial or disciplinary action occurred unless it somehow becomes a matter of public record. If an allegation is not sustained, reporters may be given some explanation for that conclusion.

Reporters have the responsibility to present their concerns in good faith. This means they may not make allegations they know to be untrue. Similarly, a reporter may not ignore or disregard information they know, or could learn upon reasonable inquiry, would tend to show the allegation is untrue. Reporters should not make frivolous allegations. That is, they should not seek a workplace investigation of matters a reasonable person would know do not constitute violations of law, rule, or regulation, or other matters appropriate for workplace investigation. Otherwise, and to protect the integrity of the investigation process, the reporter is subject to disciplinary action.

### *Witnesses*

Witnesses are the people you choose to interview because they may have information that tends to support or refute an allegation, or information that may lead to the discovery of such information. Most people are selected as witnesses because they have knowledge of the facts surrounding an allegation. Witnesses may be able to provide first-hand, indirect, or circumstantial, evidence.

Witnesses are divided into two categories for the purpose of selecting appropriate interviewing techniques. Cooperating witnesses are those who are willing to assist the investigator's attempts to develop pertinent facts. For example, when asked, they usually will tell a narrative story that requires minimal questioning, and therefore may be interviewed using standard interviewing techniques. Hostile witnesses are reluctant or unwilling to cooperate with the investigator. Often, you use interrogation techniques, such as asking questions that require only a yes or no answer.

Witnesses may become implicated people during the course of an investigation. You must be alert to ensure their rights (and those of the company to take action against them in appropriate cases) are protected should that happen. Witnesses may not be subjected to retaliation for cooperating with a workplace investigation.

### *Implicated People*

Implicated people are employees against whom an allegation of misconduct has been made. Implicated people should be given the opportunity to comment on, respond to, or rebut the allegations made against them. The investigation should not be considered complete until you have obtained the implicated person's version of the events in question. (Exceptions, however, include where the implicated person has already resigned or refuses to cooperate with the inquiries.) This information may aid your determination of what actually happened. In addition, information provided by the implicated person may assist the responsible managers in determining what action, if any, to take against the implicated person. For example, when you conclude that the implicated person violated an applicable standard, you should try to determine whether the violation was due to ignorance of, inability to comply with, or deliberate disregard for, the standard.

### *Probable Cause to Investigate*

Generally speaking, employees should be left alone to do their jobs. Even though an investigation may be needed from time to time, an investigation should never be a "fishing expedition" in order to locate some elusive misconduct believed to be lurking around your company.

You have limited corporate authority. An investigation may not be opened indiscriminately. Similarly, a reporter does not have the right to insist on an investigation simply because your company has an investigation function or promotes its hotline. An investigation is appropriate—and your authority kicks in—only if the initial report gives you probable cause to believe that misconduct has occurred. Never make any promises or commitments that action will be taken, other than that the information will be looked into.

What is probable cause? Probable cause is a criminal-justice concept. It reflects the value judgment that people are entitled to be free from scrutiny unless some basic factual threshold is satisfied. Probable cause means (i) that you reasonably believe a violation of your code of conduct, law or regulation may have occurred in your workplace, and (ii) you reasonably believe that the named employee committed it. If you have probable cause, an investigation is proper. Otherwise, an investigation is not appropriate at that time. (However, if later facts establish the probable cause, than an investigation should be opened.)

### *Degree of Proof Required*

To be fair to the employees implicated in your investigation, you have a burden of proof to satisfy. This means that you have to gather evidence to substantiate each element of the misconduct allegedly committed.

Once the evidence has been gathered, it has to be measured against a standard of proof. This is whether you have gathered enough proof to consider the allegation to be substantiated.

The applicable standard of proof in a workplace investigation is a "preponderance of the evidence." An allegation is considered proven if, based on the facts learned and the documents reviewed, it is more likely than not—think 51 percent or more—that the misconduct actually happened. If so, the allegation is considered substantiated. If not, the allegation is considered unsubstantiated.

The preponderance-of-the-evidence standard is not a criminal-justice standard. The criminal-justice standard, as you likely know, is "beyond a reasonable doubt." This means that the proof makes it at least 90 percent certain that the misconduct actually happened. This is another reason why the right to remain silent and the right to a lawyer—both constitutional rights in criminal cases—don't apply to employees in workplace investigations.

This topic underscores why you should avoid criminal-justice concepts and standards in your investigations. For example, if you adopted the beyond-a-reasonable-doubt standard, this would force you, among other things, to spend more resources and time than needed. It will also result in substantiated misconduct going unpunished when you cannot meet a 90 percent standard, although you satisfied the 51 percent standard that did apply.

## *Rights to Protect Privacy and Reputation*

Allegations resulting in workplace investigations usually involve sensitive issues, impact the implicated person's department, are against people in positions of responsibility and trust, and are derogatory in nature. Consequently, the mere existence of an allegation may constitute an invasion of privacy, harm the reputation and careers of individuals, and tarnish the image of a manager. The files that reflect such investigations are retained long after an investigation is completed, regardless of the results. They have serious implications for the privacy rights of participants.

Everyone you interview should be informed that the information they provide will be maintained in files used for official purposes (including the investigation itself and any prosecution or disciplinary action that may result), and that access to the information within the company will be on a "need to know" basis. In addition, the information may be used in some situations to respond to complaints or requests for information from government agencies, including state and local law-enforcement agencies.

## *Expectations of Confidentiality*

Many people who participate in workplace investigations think their identity and the nature of their contact will be maintained in strict confidence. In fact, there is no absolute right to confidentiality, and the responsibilities of a workplace occasionally require some disclosure of sources of information. Consequently, you should never state or imply that confidentiality is an "absolute" or "unqualified" right that will be protected under all conditions. Such a promise is misleading because disclosure may be required to accomplish a legitimate business purpose or compelled by law in certain cases.

Confidentiality creates a dilemma for the investigation process. On the one hand, an expectation of confidentiality increases the likelihood reporters will report their concerns and makes witnesses more willing to cooperate with a workplace investigation. On the other hand, as the information a workplace investigation is able to provide responsible managers about the source of facts decreases, so does the credibility of the presentation and the likelihood that action will be taken in response to the investigation. Also, as the severity of the action taken in response to an investigation increases, so does the demand for disclosure of sources. For example, a department may decide to take corrective action—steps that will fix an actual or perceived deficiency in the way it conducts business—even when the investigative facts come from reporters and key witnesses who insist upon confidentiality.

There are two kinds of confidentiality: *express* and *implied*.

## *Implied Confidentiality*

A limited degree of confidentiality is generally given to all reporters under your code of conduct. Reporters are assured confidentiality to encourage full disclosure of information without fear of retaliation. Normally, hotline users are encouraged to identify themselves so that additional facts can be obtained if necessary. In those instances where you learn the identity of a previously anonymous reporter, it should be protected to the extent possible.

Implied confidentiality applies to all reporters and witnesses, whether or not they request it. Implied confidentiality means that you are required to take reasonable steps to avoid disclosing the identity of reporters and witnesses until the investigation is completed and management has decided whether or not disciplinary action is appropriate. At that point, the protection afforded by implied confidentiality ends if the decision is to take disciplinary action, because the identities are required for the official purpose of pursuing disciplinary action.

You should not reveal the names of reporters or witnesses to anyone unless it is necessary for the successful completion of the investigation. In particular, be careful not to reveal the source of information you discuss with the implicated person or implicated person's department until the investigation is completed and the investigative report has been issued. On rare occasions, however, it may become necessary to confront one witness with the statements made by another witness in order to determine credibility or resolve conflicting evidence presented by them. You may provide the names of witnesses (but not reporters) to management at the conclusion of the investigation. Indeed, the investigative report will identify all witnesses who have not been given an express grant of confidentiality. However, you should not provide the underlying documentation (interview memoranda, investigator notes, etc.) to management unless the materials are specifically requested.

You should not provide information to the implicated person's department or the responsible managers indicating the identity of the reporter without first discussing it with the reporter. If the reporter has first-hand knowledge and is interviewed as a witness, the investigative notes and the report should treat the information provided in the same manner as any other witness. If the reporter has no first-hand knowledge and is not interviewed as a witness, neither the implicated person's department nor the responsible manager have a significant need to know the source of the report.

## *Express Grant of Confidentiality*

An express grant of confidentiality occurs when you tell sources such as reporters or witnesses that their identity or the information they provide will receive more extensive protection than implied confidentiality. Generally, this happens when you say that the identity of a reporter will not be revealed to responsible managers at the end of the investigation. Because there can never be an absolute or complete grant of confidentiality, an investigator who makes a promise that exceeds the limits of implied confidentiality may find the only way to keep that promise is to delete from the investigative report all references to the identity of the reporter to whom the promise was made, and to information provided by that reporter which cannot be obtained from another source.

In some cases, such as when an allegation is serious and discipline is likely to result if it is sustained, it may become necessary to refrain from making any written record of the identity of the reporter in order to keep the promise. Because this greatly limits the use to which information provided by the reporter may be used, you should rarely give an express grant of confidentiality to a witness. It is more common to give express grants of confidentiality to reporters. However, you should be especially cautious when the reporter seeks redress of a personal injury, as it may be difficult to correct the wrong without identifying the reporter at some point in the process.

Information provided under an express grant of confidentiality may prove helpful for taking corrective or remedial action. However, when disciplinary action is likely to result, the investigator should anticipate such information will be useful only for the purpose of developing leads. Because witnesses may be compelled to answer your questions, express confidentiality should be granted to witnesses only when you have come to a dead end and believe the grant would make a witness more candid or helpful in developing useful leads the investigator could pursue with other witnesses.

An express grant of confidentiality may encourage a reporter to present allegations and supporting facts that otherwise would remain unknown. However, a promise of express confidentiality should be made only after a specific request by the reporter to whom implied confidentiality has been fully explained. You may decline to give an express grant of confidentiality, in which case reporters must decide whether to provide information under the implied confidentiality standard.

Once an express grant of confidentiality is provided, an appropriate note should be placed in the investigative file. Express grants of confidentiality are subject to renegotiation. As the investigation develops, you may find that the allegation cannot be sustained, or disciplinary action supported, unless sources who have been granted express confidentiality agree to be identified.

However, when doing so, you must take care not to appear to be making a threat to reveal the identity of the source without consent. In deciding whether to give an express grant of confidentiality, you should consider the following factors:

- The seriousness of the allegation;
- The likelihood the witness may be subject to retaliation or other harm should the source of the information become known to the implicated person or other persons who do not want the matter investigated;
- The ability of the company to protect the witness from retaliation (consider, for example, the difference between private sector employees who are entitled to statutory "whistleblower" protection and those who are not);

- The importance to the investigation of the information the witness is able to provide; and
- The likelihood the investigator would be able to develop the information through other sources.

Whenever you give an express grant of confidentiality, an investigator must include a warning that the grant may be overturned by public authorities in appropriate circumstances and that consequently, there can be no "guarantee" of, or "absolute right" to, confidentiality. Although express grants of confidentiality are discouraged, there are occasions where they may be useful to both an investigator and the reporter. If the reporter can provide leads sufficient that you do not need to rely upon information that only the reporter can provide, the investigation may be successfully completed and the reporter may be able to avoid subsequent identification by the implicated person or others. Because information provided only by the reporter would not be used to take action against the reporter, it should be possible to protect the identity of the reporter from release during disciplinary proceedings.

## *Rights against Retaliation*

Reporters and witnesses who seek confidentiality usually fear retaliation. The right to communicate a concern of actual or possible misconduct free from fear of retaliation is essential to a proper workplace and critical to an effective workplace investigation process. It should be discussed with reporters and witnesses who express concerns about confidentiality. You should discuss this right with implicated people and implicated persons' departments when they are notified of a workplace investigation.

Some reporters and witnesses have a statutory right to be free from retaliation for disclosing information or otherwise cooperating with a workplace investigation. For example, most employees are protected from retaliation for "blowing the whistle," since enactment of whistleblower statutes. These whistleblower statutes contain limitations on the type of information that may be disclosed, the persons to whom a protected disclosure may be made, and the type of conduct that constitutes retaliation. Disclosures of the type of information that would be of interest to a workplace organization are generally covered, and investigators are included in the categories of persons to whom protected disclosures may be made.

Your company should have a policy providing that people who make good-faith disclosures of suspected misconduct to "proper managers" will be protected from retaliation of any kind. Employees in the management chain of command are generally considered proper managers.

However, whistleblower protection does not extend to employees who disclosed information with the knowledge that it was false or with willful disregard for its truth or falsity. Under those circumstances, the disclosure is not made in good faith (note, however, an allegation may be made in good faith even if it is not sustained, or is demonstrated to have been wrong). Also, frivolous allegations (allegations of facts that would not constitute misconduct even if true) may be made in good faith by people who misunderstand the applicable standards. Continued persistence in asserting such allegations after the standards have been explained need not be regarded as made in good faith.

Investigators who become aware of threats or acts that could constitute retaliation against personnel cooperating in an investigation should immediately document their information and advise their superiors. The investigators and/or their superiors should then make further inquiries.

### *An Investigator's Right of Access*

Investigators are entitled to reasonable access to people, places, and documents necessary to conduct the investigation. No employee should withhold company records from anyone authorized to have access to them. Access problems that cannot be resolved at the local level should be escalated up the investigator's management chain for resolution.

### *A Witness's Right to Know Status*

Investigators are generally not required to inform witnesses of their interview status (witness or implicated person). However, you may advise witnesses of their status, and that is usually done so in order to facilitate the interview. You should anticipate that people will ask whether they are accused or suspected of any wrongdoing at the outset of the interview. If asked, you should reveal the witness's current status, along with a statement that the status may change as the investigation continues and additional facts are learned.

### Right to Consult with a Lawyer

An employee who is either a witness or implicated person has no right to consult with counsel as part of that employee's participation in a workplace investigation.

### Duty to Cooperate with the Investigation

Employees have a duty to cooperate with a workplace investigation. Employees should be required to report suspected fraud and misconduct. These provisions may be used to compel the employees to answer questions or face disciplinary action (including dismissal).

### Right to Have Counsel Present

Employees do not have this right, but you may permit counsel to attend the interview. This may make the witness more comfortable and cooperative, and therefore help you. You should take reasonable steps to ensure that counsel does not interfere with the interview.

### Right to Have Others Present

Witnesses may ask to have a friend or family member present during questioning. Although there is no right to have such people present, you may permit this if it would appear to facilitate the interview. You must be vigilant to ensure the privacy interests of third parties will not be violated. Observers should also be told to take no role in the interview, such as speaking to the witness.

### Right to Comment on Adverse Information

Implicated people generally have no specific right to comment on or rebut adverse information about them. However, considerations of fairness and prudence often lead an investigator to give them this opportunity. It is not necessary to make all unfavorable allegations or information known to them. Generally, allegations not deemed worthy of investigation should not be revealed. Conversely, allegations that appear to be substantiated should be revealed, and the implicated person should be allowed the opportunity to comment on them specifically. They should also be informed of, and permitted to comment upon, any other derogatory information that will be maintained in the investigative file. Comments may take the form of:

- Oral responses made during the course of an interview;
- Sworn or unsworn written statements proffered by the implicated person;
- Documents or physical evidence; and
- A request that you interview others the implicated person or suspect asserts may have pertinent information the investigator should consider.

In most cases, implicated people should be interviewed near the end of the investigation, after all adverse information has been developed. In some cases, it may be advisable to interview them at an early stage of the investigation, as when they may be the only source of certain information necessary in the preliminary stages of an investigation. You should advise them, however, that they may be interviewed more extensively at a later date.

### *Right to Ensure Investigative Accuracy*

You must ensure the accuracy of the information contained in the investigative report. Similarly, the investigation needs to convince others that information is accurate should it be challenged after the investigative report is issued. The most likely source of such a challenge is the witness who claims that you did not accurately record what the witness said. Before, during, and after the interview, witnesses who are likely to raise such challenges may express concern over their ability to ensure you accurately record the information they provide. At times, they may request to make a tape recording of the interview, to review the notes you took during the interview, or to read your interview memo. Witnesses have no right to do any of these things. However, the prudent investigator can use the witness's concern as a tool to preclude subsequent challenge.

Therefore, to ensure accuracy, you should consider the following steps when these concerns have arisen or are expected to arise:

- You could review your notes with the witness before completing the interview. Witnesses who believe that you took accurate notes are less likely to ask to see a copy of your interview memo. You have the discretion to ask witnesses to read and comment upon a draft result of the interview report, and should do so in appropriate cases. This is especially important when the witness provides technical or complex information.

- Consider asking the witness to provide a sworn or unsworn written statement. The accuracy of the information in such documents is less subject to dispute than the report, and the documents may be used to impeach a person who later tries to change the story. Some investigators believe every witness who has information material to the proof or refutation of an allegation should be asked to provide a sworn statement. Witnesses who are concerned about the accuracy of the report should also be offered the opportunity to give a sworn or unsworn written statement.
- When you are concerned the witness will recant in the time between the interview and the preparation of the document memorializing it (investigator's report or signed witness statement), you should prepare the interview memorandum immediately after the interview.
- In extreme cases, you may wish to tape the interview, and play back answers to specific questions when the witness does not agree with your written characterization of the response.

If making a tape recording is essential to obtaining the interview (as, for example in the case of a third-party witness who cannot be ordered to cooperate), you may be able to convince the witness to give you the tape until completion of the investigation. At the completion of the investigation, it is acceptable to give witnesses copies of their sworn or unsworn written statements upon request. In dealing with these issues, you should keep in mind that the objective, ensuring accuracy, is of equal concern to the company as to the witness.

## *Right to Know Results and to Review the Report*

Reporters, witnesses and implicated people have no inherent right to know the outcome of an investigation or to review any final investigative report that may be issued pursuant to an investigation. However, your company may choose to apprise reporters of the general results of an investigation. Fairness dictates that implicated people should be afforded the same courtesy.

Reporters and witnesses have no greater right to review a copy of the final investigative report than do members of the general public. These materials should not be provided to implicated people or suspects directly in those cases, but should work through counsel assigned to handle the matter.

# PART II
## Conducting the Workplace Investigation

Now to the "nuts and bolts" of a workplace investigation: An important rule is that you must "own" your investigations. You determine the manner in which the investigations will be conducted. Considering the goals, views and concerns of management is important, but you determine the investigation's particulars.

> **Process Pointer:** Just like any other business process, this one has to be implemented fairly. Fairness for everyone is critical, especially for the implicated person because he has the most at risk. "Owning" an investigation is the gold standard between a professional and a hack investigator. If you act as if you own the investigation, you are poised to offer true value to your company.

## A) The Four Critical Steps
A properly conducted workplace investigation follows four steps:
   1. **Determine the nature of the allegation.** You must gain a quick understanding of the problem. Usually, someone in the company knows the subject matter at issue and might even have personal knowledge of the incident. That person must be quickly debriefed so that you have some basis from which to proceed and a solid idea of how the matter under investigation evolved.

2. **Develop the Facts.** There are two basic components to the fact development in a workplace investigation: interviews of employees or third parties, and the review of relevant documents. Document review is an important part of any investigation. Documents provide a historical narrative of events. They often tell much of the story by themselves. Also, they can provide a written framework into which information developed through witness interviews will fit.

3. **Document the Investigation.** To serve as a basis for management decisions, the investigation findings must be documented and supported. The report must give a comprehensive explanation of the information gathered in the course of the investigation. Sometimes a brief memorandum will suffice. In a complex investigation, a detailed written report will be prepared for presentation to executive management. The complexity of the issues and the stakes involved often dictate the way the investigation is documented.

4. **Publish the Findings.** Once completed, the investigation findings must be disclosed to management, the reporter and the implicated person. Of course, the level of detail will vary as necessary as will the document you produce, if at all, to each of them.

## B) Understanding the Initial Report

Reports will come to you from a number of internal and external sources. (For convenience, we will assume the report came in through the company's whistleblower hotline.) Regardless of its source, you need sufficient information to provide probable cause that misconduct may have occurred. If so, then sufficient reason exists to begin an investigation. You should examine the initially available facts to determine if either the source of the information or the combination of the source of the information and the then-available facts offer probable cause.

### Meeting the Reporter

Consider the form of the report. Was it anonymous, or did it come from an identified party? Anonymous reports should not be discounted unfairly. An anonymous report may be malicious, or it may be valid and accurate. Some employees do not trust management to keep their names confidential. Some do not want to be identified as the person responsible for bringing the matter to the attention of management. The detail provided in the anonymous report, or the lack of it, may either validate or invalidate the report. Keep an open mind and don't jump to conclusions either way.

> **Process Pointer:** Your company must accept anonymous complaints because you want maximum feedback on how your employees are acting improperly. You need to remain attentive if someone tells you, even anonymously, that one of your employees could be engaging in misconduct.

Reporters who speak to a hotline caseworker or investigator are submitting themselves to the interview process at that time. Under ideal circumstances, reporter interviews are conducted by the person who also conducts the principal investigation. As this is not always practical, those people doing initial reporter interviews should approach them as if they were going to do the principal investigation. Note that no matter how thorough the initial interview may be, the person eventually assigned to conduct the principal investigation should also interview the reporter whenever possible. When reporters insist on anonymity, consider asking them to call back at some later date to receive information that will enable them to contact the investigator assigned to the case.

The following points are particularly important for investigators to keep in mind when dealing with reporters:
- Set the stage for a productive interview.
- Meet walk-ins in a semi-private area that permits initial assessment and control of security and safety. Then move to a comfortable, private area that will encourage the reporter to be completely candid during the interview.
- Use the same number of interviewers and other precautionary measures as would be appropriate for a witness interview.
- Establish good rapport; engage in active listening; and assess demeanor, candor, bias, intelligence, motivation and understanding of the implicated person, the matter, and the applicable rules.

- Encourage reporters to provide a narrative recital of their concerns with minimum interruption for questions.
- Be alert for the possibility that reporters may implicate themselves in wrongdoing.
- After listening to the narrative, ask clarifying questions, then summarize the key points. Work on the summary until the reporter agrees it is accurate and that you understand the information the reporter is trying to convey. Then write down the key points.
- Your goal is to prepare a "mini hotline report," which, as much as possible, answers the following familiar questions framed in the context of one or more allegations that would be appropriate for a workplace investigation:
    1. Who engaged in the wrongdoing?
    2. What did they do (or fail to do) that constitutes the wrongdoing?
    3. What standard, rule, regulation, law, etc. was violated when this happened?
    4. When did this happen?
    5. Where did it happen?
    6. How did it happen?
    7. Why does the reporter think this happened, i.e., was it intentional, negligent, a lack of training, a motive of personal gain or an intent to injure another, etc?
    8. How is the company adversely affected by what happened?
    9. Who was harmed by what happened, and in what manner?
    10. What corrective remedial, or disciplinary action, if any, does the reporter think should be taken, and why?
- Probe for weaknesses by asking reporters to explain what they expect the person implicated in their allegations or others who might not agree with the reporter would say in defense of their actions, and why such a response is not sufficient to dispose of the matter.
- Ask reporters to identify others who may have pertinent information about the matter that would tend to support or refute the reporter's position. Ask reporters to identify documents that relate to the matter, including those that would tend to support or refute the

reporter's position, and, if possible, to provide copies of them for the investigative file as soon as possible.

- Ask reporters who else they may have contacted in an attempt to get action on their complaints, and what those others have done to date.
- Ask reporters what they want the company to do about their report. This helps to focus the report and permits a determination of whether the case should be referred to another department. It also provides an opportunity to tell reporters whether their expectations are realistic, in regards to what you can or will do.
- Get as much detailed information as possible. A detailed first discussion helps to prepare a good, efficient investigation plan and reduces the number of times you may need to contact the reporter for more information.
- Don't express opinions about the alleged conduct, and avoid opinions or comments about the character or ability of the others involved.
- Advise the reporter not to discuss the matter with others within the company except those with a need to know.
- Reassure the reporter that the company takes these complaints seriously and will determine whether an investigation is needed. Emphasize that no final conclusion will be reached until the investigation has been completed.
- If the reporter asks whether he will receive a copy of a final report of the investigation, the reporter should be informed that, although a final report will be prepared, the reporter will not receive a copy. Similarly, no specific, detailed report will be made to the reporter on management's response to the allegation.
- Advise the reporter to immediately report any possible acts of retaliation.
- Explain that, depending on the information that is learned, the investigation may be resolved at an informal stage rather than through a formal investigation.
- If the reporter says that he only wants to share his concerns but does not want an investigation conducted, inform the reporter that, depending on the information, your company may have a legal obligation to investigate the report.

> **Process Pointer:** Don't accept the reporter's characterization of the allegation at face value. You must analyze the facts you are offered and make your own determination regarding the category in which it fits. The report from the person who made the allegation is just a report. Offer no opinions to the reporter. At that time, you probably don't know the motives, personalities or histories of the people involved.

## *Discuss Confidentiality*

If asked, most employees would say they assume the identities of hotline reporters are maintained in confidence. This may explain why reporters never ask whether their identity will be protected. The ability to identify reporters to responsible managers and use them as witnesses in adverse actions enhances the likelihood of a successful investigation. Therefore, you should discuss this matter with reporters and document their wishes.

An explanation of the normal practice regarding (implied) confidentiality includes:

- The identity of the reporter, as such, is generally not provided to anyone other than those with a need to know. Reporters who seek redress of injuries that are personal to them will probably need to be identified to the implicated person's department at some point during the investigative process in order to correct the injury.
- If the reporter has first-hand knowledge of the matter to be investigated, the initial interview, or a subsequent interview, may be treated as an ordinary witness interview, in which case the reporter will be identified as a witness in the investigative report, and perhaps during the course of the investigation should it become necessary to reconcile conflicting witness statements.
- The reporter's identity is usually furnished to the investigator. If the reporter objects to such disclosure, the reporter's name should be released to the investigator, but this may limit the investigator's ability to conduct the investigation or substantiate the allegations. Since some reporters do not mind being identified, determine and document whether the reporter is willing to be identified as the reporter:
    1. To the investigator assigned to handle the case;
    2. To the responsible manager;

3. To the implicated person's department; and
4. To the implicated person of the investigation.

Affirmative responses may assist the investigator assigned the case.

Finally, it should be explained that if the implicated person is disciplined as a result of the investigation and brings a lawsuit, then the implicated person will normally be entitled to review the entire case file, including information that may identify the reporter, after that action is taken. If the reporter objects, then the investigator may wish to discuss conditions of express confidentiality. If the investigator and reporter agree to an express grant of confidentiality, the investigator must document the terms of the agreement for the case file and take appropriate action to ensure it is honored.

In some cases, reporters will ask for an explanation of the company's policy on confidentiality at the start of the conversation. You must not promise complete or absolute confidentiality because there is no way to ensure it in all circumstances. When reporters are granted some degree of express confidentiality, they may be assigned a "confidential source number" and referred to by that number in all case documents and reports.

## *Granting Anonymity*

Some reporters refuse to provide their names or a means of contacting them during the course of a phone or face-to-face interview. Others provide such information, and then wish they had not after they understand the consequences of filing their report. People in the first category, along with those who write unsigned letters or leave messages on answering machines without providing their names, are truly anonymous. People in the second category are not, since their identity is known to the person taking the report. However, the person taking the report may elect to treat these people as anonymous reporters by deleting all identifying information from the case file before forwarding it for further action. This action should not be taken lightly, but the interest of promoting confidence in the hotline system suggests this action is appropriate in some cases. It is especially important when the reporter expresses credible fears of retaliation. When the person taking the reports decides to grant anonymity, he should give reporters a code number and log it in the case file so reporters who later may need to prove they were the source of the report will have a means of doing so.

### Discuss Retaliation

People who seek confidentiality usually fear retaliation. The person taking the reports should probe whether reporters have any specific reason to believe they may become the targets of retaliation, and should document those fears in the case file. The person taking the reports should explain the company's policy against retaliation, being careful to point out the company cannot guarantee there will be no act of retaliation, but can take action to undo it and punish those who engage in retaliation.

### Discuss the Reporter's Role as a Witness

If reporters who are concerned about confidentiality would appear to be logical witnesses in an investigation into the report, explain there is a possibility they may be interviewed at the same time as other witnesses. This may occur inadvertently if you do not know the identity of the reporter. But investigators who know the reporter's identity may decide it necessary to interview him again to reduce the likelihood the reporter may be perceived as the original source of the report because not interviewing him along with others in the office would arouse suspicion.

### Obtaining a Written Statement

In some cases, it may be appropriate to ask the reporter to provide a written statement of the allegations and supporting facts. The writing process may assist the reporter in remembering to provide additional pertinent facts. A written report is useful if you intend to refer the investigation to another department or a government agency. The person taking the report should also consider whether to ask the reporter to provide a sworn statement. This is important when serious misconduct by senior officials is alleged. If the reporter agrees to give a statement, the interviewer should take it at that time, even if the reporter expresses a willingness to be interviewed later, to avoid the possibility the reporter may subsequently decline to give the statement. Later, the principal investigator assigned to the case can ask the reporter to prepare a second statement if it becomes necessary.

### Do Not Promise an Investigation

No promises or commitments should be made about the action that will be taken, other than that the allegations will be looked into, and, when appropriate, that a response will be provided to the reporter. After the interview is completed, you should record impressions of the reporter's understanding of the issues, attitude, apparent sincerity, credibility, and veracity in a separate document for the case file.

> **Process Pointer:** A failure to understand the complaint fully (what it includes and what it does not) can result in: a failure to investigate; a failure to investigate the right thing; a failure to talk to the right people; a failure to reach the right conclusion; and an over-reaction or under-reaction to the complaint. Do whatever it takes to get the story.

## C) Inquiry or Investigation?

The purpose of a workplace investigation is to obtain facts sufficient to enable responsible managers to make informed decisions about corrective, remedial, or disciplinary action. Some degree of stigma attaches to the implicated person in every workplace investigation, even when the allegations are not substantiated. Not all concerns reported are appropriate for a workplace investigation. Therefore, the purpose of a preliminary inquiry is to gather sufficient information to determine whether a full workplace investigation is appropriate. The inquiry should be conducted in a way that has the least adverse impact on the reputation of implicated people and their departments.

### *Preliminary Inquiries*

The preliminary inquiry is less formal than the principal investigation because it does not require the creation of a written investigative plan or the preparation of an investigative report. There is, however, no clear line dividing the preliminary inquiry from the principal investigation. Certainly, when it becomes necessary to notify the implicated person or the implicated person's department that allegations have been made against them, the preliminary inquiry is over. Also, once it becomes necessary to interview witnesses who work with the implicated person on a regular basis, and who will learn the implicated person is under investigation by the nature of the interview questions, the principal investigation has started—whether or not the implicated person has been notified. But actions that do not cross the line include: conversations with Human Resources, business executives, and legal advisors, a discrete review of applicable documents or other records, and interviews of a limited nature, in person or over the phone, especially when they are not conducted at the site of the implicated person's department.

A somewhat arbitrary dividing line is established at the point of preparation of the initial written investigative plan, which thus becomes the first step in the principal investigation. Because experience shows that reporters should be interviewed at the beginning of an investigation whenever possible, and that those interviews sometimes reveal no further investigation is necessary, the reporter interview is generally considered as part of the preliminary inquiry. Therefore it may be conducted before the written investigative plan is prepared.

When a preliminary inquiry results in a decision that no further action is warranted, neither an investigative plan nor an investigative report is required. A memorandum for the record is sufficient to document the reasons for the decision to go no further. This minimizes the number of documents in the record that may be subject to disclosure, and therefore helps minimize the adverse impact on the privacy and reputations of implicated people and others involved in the inquiry. Similarly, when the preliminary inquiry results in a referral to another company department for action, a memorandum is sufficient to close out compliance department action on the matter, unless there is a specific reason for the compliance department to continue to monitor the case.

## *Deciding to Investigate*

If you decide that a formal investigation is needed, you must answer some important questions. What will be the scope of the investigation? Who will conduct it? How much will it cost? The answers to these questions are not trivial because your responses may likely be viewed with hindsight by executive management, the press, the courts, and possibly the government.

There are certain benefits to deciding in favor of an investigation. These benefits include:
- A workplace investigation helps the company determine the extent of potential criminal or civil liability.
- If a company effectively investigates its own misconduct, the company may persuade the government to forego conducting a separate

investigation, reduce the scope of its investigation, or allow the corporation to guide the government's investigation. A credible investigation may prevent a wide-ranging government investigation into the company's affairs.
- A director's fiduciary duty to the company includes the obligation to self-police, to establish compliance and detection programs.
- When there is a duty to investigate, the failure to do so may subject management to civil liability.
- The best way to avoid indictment is to have full knowledge of all of the relevant facts so that an appropriate pre-indictment defense may be presented to the government. A thorough investigation, combined with voluntary disclosure, may be the dispositive factor in convincing the government not to bring criminal charges.
- A company can use a workplace investigation to minimize the effect of negative publicity that has arisen from allegations of wrongdoing. An investigation enhances the company's credibility now and in the future. The investigation distances the company from any wrongful acts by its employees, and the very existence of an investigation shows the company's good faith.
- A company may decide to investigate to encourage investor confidence and protect its position in the market. When allegations of misconduct are raised, the investigation may be used to address issues or dispel a cloud of suspicion.

However, consider the consequences of investigating the report. The investigation will require the commitment of time, resources and corporate energy, perhaps more than was initially expected or budgeted. There will be lost productivity in the business. People helping you will be diverted from their job duties. The internal machinery of the company will be explored and exposed. Executive management will have to live with the results of the investigation. This might include findings of fault, require public disclosure of the conduct, or the taking of internal or external remedial action.

## *Deciding Not to Investigate*

Not every allegation of misconduct must be investigated. If initial inquiries about the report fail to confirm that an incident may have occurred or that there is a commercially reasonable basis for the conduct alleged in the report, there may be no basis for an investigation at that time. For example, an investigation is not needed if:

- The report is a misunderstanding of company policy;
- The allegation relates to a lack of communication between the reporter and another person;
- No other facts are necessary to resolve the issue, or the material facts are undisputed;
- The substance of the report can be resolved informally, such as a request for assistance rather than an allegation of misconduct.

You must document the report and the basis not to proceed. The record should show that, although no investigation was made, the reasons for not proceeding were commercially reasonable. If the investigation process is audited at some later time, the permanent record documents the handling of the matter and the inquiries you made at that time. The ability to account for all inquiries made is part of the ability to build a perception in management that there is a high degree of integrity in your process. The documented decision also allows you to reopen the investigation if additional facts are obtained in the future that warrant further inquiries.

> **Process Pointer:** All the allegations must be documented or it will look as if you just pick and choose your investigations. If you choose not to investigate a report, you must document that fact and the reasons why you are not investigating.

### *Opening a Case over Objection*

Once reporters have contacted a company manager or relevant department, a business process has started. That process includes advising managers—who are also company fiduciaries—that the company may be exposed to an unacceptable business risk (usually with financial and/or legal implications). The company must look into the report and, if needed, take action to protect its employees and shareholders. Consequently, reporters have no right to insist a case file not be opened on a matter. Nor do they have the right to "withdraw" the report during an investigation and demand that an investigation be closed at that point. If there is a basis to proceed, an investigation must begin regardless of the reporter's preferences.

## *Informing Management*

When an investigation will be conducted, you should inform your management. Because workplace investigations are just another internal process, do not work secretly, unless the circumstances of the investigation are so sensitive that there is no practical alternative. The investigative function will not be accepted by the managers you must cultivate as corporate allies if you are perceived as some secret police force snooping around unannounced. Similarly, you should be mindful of the effect on the future viability of your function if your secret steps cause employees to believe they are working in some corporate "police state." A template notification memorandum for the affected business people may be found in Appendix H.

Selecting which managers to inform is not based solely on finding someone who is not involved in the matter under investigation. A senior manager of the business group involved should be informed about the nature of the investigation and its likely scope because, after all, he or she will be held accountable for your findings. The manager informed must also be of sufficient seniority to support the investigation's goals and neutralize any attempts by other managers to interfere with or impede the goals of the investigation. A sufficiently senior manager can also use their position to facilitate the availability of witnesses and the production of relevant documents. The manager informed should also be someone who will determine the action to be taken once the investigation's findings are disclosed. Consider who else in the company has a vested interest in the investigation and its outcome, such as legal counsel, Human Resources or your company's security department. (If the allegation is serious enough, consider also informing your communications and investor relations departments.)

When informing management, a detailed explanation of your investigation plan is not necessary. However, alert them when significant events happen or if the scope of the investigation changes. Tell them about key investigative issues, especially those which have the potential to be provocative or embarrassing. This will allow managers time to prepare some internal response to those issues when challenged, and it will start them thinking about the possible impact of the investigation findings on their business's operations and structure.

You and management should have a clear understanding of what they hope the investigation will accomplish. Managing expectations is a crucial part of cultivating a relationship of confidence and value.

> **Process Pointer:** Manage the expectations of the business leaders carefully. Their perceptions of the investigation, the process and your involvement will depend on it. Counsel them regarding likely outcomes, so they can prepare themselves accordingly.

### Secure the Documents

The news that an investigation has begun may spread throughout the affected business group. It might even become public knowledge. If the misconduct under investigation is likely to be proven, some employees may be tempted to destroy documents or computer files that show their involvement. Of course, your investigation will be compromised if this happens.

At the initial stages of the investigation, try to identify, with the help of the reporter if possible, the documents that are relevant to the investigation and the likely sources for those documents. Obtain the documents immediately.

Computer files should be immediately safeguarded. Consult your company's information-technology department to determine whether and to what extent server backups are done. Consider curtailing or shutting off access to company systems—or copying their system use—by employees under investigation.

## D) Planning the Investigation

### Issue Spotting

Issue spotting is the process of reviewing the facts to determine whether they would provide the basis for a management decision to take corrective, remedial, or disciplinary action. Such a determination might be based on the currently known facts alone, or it might rely on the currently known facts together with others that may be established upon further investigation.

### Looking for Misconduct Issues

Careful planning is critical to a successful, credible investigation. The issue-spotting analysis begins with the initial contact with the reporter, when you question the reporter to develop more information. It continues after the interview is completed, when you determine whether or not to open a workplace investigation. Issue spotting is the first step of the planning phase of an investigation.

Once the issues have been identified, they should be written in the form of allegations to be investigated. Consider the following:

- Do not rely on the reporter's description or characterization of the facts. You should formulate your own statement of the allegation.
- An allegation to be investigated should be expressed in neutral, non-emotional terms. It should be formulated in such a manner that substantiation (a "yes" answer) of the allegation demonstrates that misconduct has occurred.
- The allegation should be worded similar to the following: someone (the implicated person) did, or failed to do, something (the act or omission), and such act or omission was improper (the wrongdoing) because it violated some standard (law, rule, regulation, or company policy).

### *Decide What Should Be Done about Each Allegation*

Having written allegations in the proper format, you can then decide whether action is warranted and, if so, what that action should be. At this point, it may be clear that one or more of the allegations must be thoroughly investigated and discussed in a formal investigative report that documents the findings. You would then be ready to start writing the investigative plan and begin the investigation. In other cases, you may want to make discrete inquiries, which may develop additional information from other sources, before proceeding further.

Which way to proceed is a judgment call that comes with investigation experience. On the other hand, at this point you may realize that some allegations are simply not significant enough to warrant any further form of inquiry. At best, they may warrant maintaining for record purposes. If you cannot write a good allegation after consulting with others in the office, reviewing applicable policies, and perhaps talking with counsel, it may be there is nothing to investigate.

Sometimes an allegation may be serious, but contain insufficient information or detail for you to determine how to gather more information. Your company does not have sufficient resources to engage in fishing expeditions. Reports that fall in this category should be documented and closed. The matter may be reopened if and when additional information is learned.

*Developing the Investigation Plan*

You must be prepared to conduct a comprehensive, objective, fair and professional investigation. The planning needs to be flexible to accommodate new information and developments. The investigation may have to be expanded as information is developed.

The detail required, and the time consumed, to plan an investigation depends on the allegations. Routine investigations usually require a minimum amount of time and detail, and a simple outline. More complex investigations need more time and require finely developed planning.

> **Process Pointer:** A broad investigation objective is not optimal—it is more likely the sign of a poor investigation plan than a good one. Investigators who cannot narrow the objective are likely unclear regarding their precise needs, so they cast the net wider hoping to catch their objective. All you need to investigate is whether the specific allegation against a specific person can be supported by the information you learn in the investigation.

The scope of the investigation should also reinforce the fairness of the process. If the company must later defend a decision based on the investigation—a wrongful termination claim, for example—it will appear unreasonable for an employer to have reached a conclusion based on no or weak evidence. It will also appear unfair if the company disciplines an employee based on weak evidence when better or stronger evidence was reasonably available but ignored.

Proper definition of the scope also protects the innocent. A properly conducted investigation identifies culpable employees, but that does not mean that other individuals might not be injured as a result of the fact-finding. The importance of defining the scope of an investigation is, in some ways, an effort to protect the innocent, to narrowly define the area to be investigated and to assure that those not involved in a particular act of misconduct are neither implicated by their proximity to the event nor exonerated by omission. A proper investigation determines the relevant facts, provides a basis for fixing accountability, and provides a basis for neutralizing rumors and innuendo.

Once the scope has been determined, make your plan. This is more than just a list of documents and witnesses. It incorporates your proposed strategy. A proper strategy, regardless of the investigation's complexity, makes the investigation thorough and professional. The strategy of the investigation should move from the general to the specific, gradually zeroing in on the implicated person by carefully acquiring and analyzing information. As information is gathered, your theory can be refined to focus the investigation on the most logical source of misconduct and/or business process failure.

An investigation plan also ensures that the company has met its obligations to the implicated person, to the proper operations of the business, and to the company's shareholders. A good investigation plan addresses each of the following issues and questions:

- What are the alleged facts and behavior that led to the investigation? This can be set out in a chronology of events which can then be enlarged as the investigation develops.
- Which company employees are the subject of the investigation?
- What law, policies, procedures, codes of conduct or other requirements may have been violated, and where can the documents specifying those requirements be located?
- How widespread is the misconduct? Is this an isolated occurrence or a systemic problem?
- What information will be sought on each issue, and who are the potential sources of that information?
- What type of report should be prepared to publish the findings?
- After the investigation is completed, what post-investigation steps are likely to be needed?
- Which individuals might have personal knowledge about one or more of the factual issues?
- In what order should the witnesses be interviewed?
- What specific issues are to be covered with each witness?
- What documents will be needed to conduct the investigation and complete the investigation file?
- What documents will be shown to each witness, and which documents will be sought from each witness?
- Which senior managers will receive the reported findings, and to whom will the investigative team report?

There may be serious consequences if the investigation is too narrow or too broad. You need to get to the root cause of the problem and not just deal with its symptoms. If the investigation is superficial, the business problem will not be addressed, and the workplace may be exposed to further disruption. However, an overly broad investigation can equally harm the workplace culture and disrupt the business.

As the investigation proceeds, be flexible to changes in the plan. Situations change, and you have to be able to adapt. The true nature of the problem under investigation may turn out to be different from what you first thought. Do not let the investigation process become so rigid that you can't alter it when necessary.

If you change the investigation objectives, it may be a good idea to add a contemporaneous note to the file documenting the new objectives and your reasons for changing them. This could help you later if you are accused of some improper motive for changing. (You must protect the process from being put on trial by the implicated person.)

> **Process Pointer:** An investigation plan does not have to be formal, but set the scope properly so you will have the right parameters to guide you. You always must be prepared to explain why you did what you did. Never put yourself in the position of explaining your plan by saying that you never considered any other course of action.

## E) Investigator Best Practices

Investigating is equal parts of art and science. The best techniques needed to investigate allegations of workplace misconduct vary, and the techniques reflect the strengths and personality of the investigator using them. However, better investigations follow similar practices:

Be fair and objective. Everyone involved in an investigation deserves to be treated with respect and dignity. This protects the legitimacy of the investigations process. Under typical circumstances, the implicated person will have a real opportunity to respond.

Remember that, in the context of an investigation, words have special meanings. An investigation is not an inquisition. The person who brings a matter to your attention is a "reporter." The report is not a complaint or claim. It is just information. If the report is made regarding someone, that person is the "implicated person," not a target. Using proper terminology reinforces your role as a business-oriented truth gatherer and not a prosecutor.

You may feel tempted to pre-judge the outcome of an investigation before all the witnesses have been interviewed and all the relevant documents have been reviewed. Healthy doubt is a good trait. But good investigators resist the temptation to jump to conclusions. It could cloud your judgment. Until the report has been proven or a suspicion validated, there has been no confirmation of wrongdoing. Nor should a report be dismissed simply based on your opinion of the source. Keep an open mind to other possible explanations or scenarios.

Be sensitive to any actual or perceived conflicts of interest that might arise when you make your inquiries. Avoid even the appearance of bias or partiality to a particular person or result. If you believe that an actual or perceived conflict exists—such as if you know the people involved in some way that might compromise your objectivity or you have some interest in the matter being investigated—stop and inform the Investigations Manager immediately.

Seek maximum cooperation from your witnesses. Full, voluntary cooperation may be hard to get, but the goal should be to get witnesses to go beyond the basics and give as complete a picture as possible. This includes suggesting other witnesses with whom to speak.

Keep the interviews serious and business-like. Investigations are a serious process. Remain calm and in control throughout the interview. There is no place for joking, sarcasm or threats. People involved in an investigation are generally apprehensive about the issues involved and their possible consequences. Recognize the significance of your work and its potential impact. People, including those in executive positions, could lose their jobs as a result of your findings.

A good interviewer never stoops to undignified tactics. At times, you may need to be aggressive or tenacious, but you should never be insulting or demeaning. There are times in an interview when you will not be treated politely. Despite the hurt and angry feelings such conduct may evoke in you, you cannot lower yourself to that level. If you become angry, insulted or offended during an interview, you give up control of the interview.

Never mislead a witness. This will result in employees distrusting the entire compliance process—exactly the opposite atmosphere you are trying to create.

Do not discuss your opinions or conclusions. The witness does not need to know what you think.

Protect the confidentiality of the investigation. Allegations of misconduct, even if later found to be groundless, may still damage someone's reputation. Do not disclose the allegations or the existence of an investigation to anyone without a need to know. Curiosity by others, including executive management, is not a basis for sharing information about an investigation. The inadvertent disclosure of information could lead to the implicated person bringing claims for defamation or infliction of emotional distress. Sensitive or confidential information should not be disclosed to witnesses during the course of the investigation.

Make the inquiries promptly, but take the time needed to exercise appropriate diligence. Make sure the inquiries are made timely to ensure that appropriate documents and e-mails are preserved, and that all steps are taken to stop continuing or imminent noncompliance.

Take all steps necessary to protect whistleblowers and those who cooperate in the investigation. Avoid disclosing to the witness the source of the report. Any report of retaliation that emerges during the investigation should be treated as an additional report of possible misconduct and reported to the Investigations Manager immediately.

When making inquiries, consider the broader implications of what you have discovered for the affected business group or the company as a whole. In addition to making recommendations to management about what, if any, action should be taken with regard to the person involved, recommend appropriate changes to policies, procedures, training, monitoring, audits, or other steps to prevent a recurrence. Before making recommendations regarding systemic changes, consider what the underlying causes of the problems were. The investigation should be used to improve the business.

> **Process Pointer:** No one expects perfection, but everyone expects fairness. Never do anything that you would not be prepared to explain to the CEO of your company and say "you're damn right I did." Prejudging the outcome also causes problems because it closes your mind to other possibilities, explanations, and participants. You could easily miss a bigger investigative picture because you were too focused on the limited scope of your current inquiry.

## F) The Personal Interview

The spoken word is usually the greatest source of investigative evidence and often is the best evidence. No investigation is complete until every material witness, implicated person, and, when possible, the reporter, has been interviewed. Proficiency in interviewing assures a high degree of accuracy in fact development, helps prove or disprove the issue at hand, prevents surprise testimony from arising later, and may help impeach witnesses who change their stories later.

The purpose of interviewing, of course, is to gather information. You do this through a process of asking and answering questions. The word "process" denotes a dynamic interaction, with many variables operating with, and acting upon, one another. To understand and effectively employ this process, you must first consider the interview as a unique form of interpersonal communication. You have one goal: reporting the objective truth. Whether you can reach that goal depends in large part on the personal attributes you bring to the interview process.

Even when interviewing cooperative witnesses, you may find it difficult to acquire all the pertinent facts the witness possesses. Most people learn to interview by "trial and error" practice on many persons or by watching other interviewers. Following or using techniques of untrained or inexperienced interviewers can lead to problems. Effective interviewing is a skill that must be learned by special training and then supplemented by the experience that comes from constant practice.

Employees are sources of valuable information to investigators. When they cooperate, they can explain relevant facts and interpret relevant documents. They can give insights into management styles and corporate cultures that put specific employee conduct into context. Sample requests for employee interviews may be found in Appendices I and J.

Information may be broadly grouped into two areas: trivial and important. The important information is the information offered in response to "who, what, where, when, why and how" questions. It also includes both unusual observations and the interviewer's gut reactions.

Interviews involve a brief relationship between two people: the interviewer and the witness. The witness, one way or another, has to be persuaded that talking to the investigator is the most important thing they should be doing at that moment.

The witness may be reluctant to provide the needed information, or to cooperate. In these situations, you have a two-step task: first, to make the subject willing to cooperate with the questioning, and secondly, to interview him. This is your challenge. There are a number of ways you may get the witness's cooperation:

- Ask general questions;
- Explain the advantages of cooperation;
- Downplay the disadvantages of cooperation
- Play on their conscience;
- Speak their language and empathize;
- Give them a chance to explain.

Whatever the methods, develop your own rapport with the witness. This creates a connection between you, and it then becomes possible to create a change in the behavior of the witness. The dynamics of rapport constitute the foundation of the inquiry-persuasion process. It allows you to enter the world of the witness.

> **Process Pointer:** Interview only those people for which you need to fill factual gaps. Decide early on what exactly you need to know and who can best give it to you. Do not look for witnesses whose information does nothing more than repeat credible information you already know. These other witnesses may have differing recollections and send you off on irrelevant tangents.

> **Process Pointer:** Before interviewing anyone, decide who likely has the information you need and who is likely to give it to you. Don't assume that everyone will cooperate and tell you the truth. People may lie or be reluctant to cooperate for a variety of motives, including nothing more than a desire not to get involved.

## *Qualities of Good Interviewers*

The qualities and personal attributes required to be a good interviewer can usually be developed with training and practice. Four of the most important qualities for success as an interviewer are:

- Honesty, integrity and the ability to impress upon all witnesses that you seek only the truth regarding the matter under investigation;
- The ability to establish rapport quickly and under diverse conditions;
- The ability to listen to witnesses and evaluate responses; and
- The ability to maintain self-control during interviews and not become emotionally involved in the investigation.

## *Planning for the Interview*

Preparation is the key to successful interviewing. You should obtain as much information as possible on the details of the case and the background, character and habits of the persons involved. This helps determine the most effective interview procedures applicable to each interview. In addition to an overall investigative plan, an effective investigator has a specific plan for the conduct of every interview.

The plan should take into account the following:

- The type of interview - subcategories of reporters and witnesses include victims, eyewitnesses, hearsay witnesses, expert witnesses and informants; each may require a slightly different approach;
- The physical and psychological factors, discussed below, to be used during the conduct of the interview;
- The questioning technique to be employed (interview or interrogation), and whether the witness will be asked to prepare for the interview, shown documents or confronted with information obtained from other witnesses;

- The outline of topics to be covered, their order, and whether it is necessary to write out specific questions to ensure they are asked precisely (especially helpful when technical issues are involved). Outlines provide clear-cut goals and objectives for the interview. Outlines describe each topic to be resolved, but usually do not include written questions that must be asked. This prevents you from focusing on reading the questions, forgetting to listen to the answers (to ensure they are responsive), and failing to ask appropriate follow-up questions.
- Whether a second investigator will be present during the interview, and the role the second investigator will play;
- The manner of recording the information developed during the interview (investigator notes and report, witness's written statement, tape recording, videotaping, or a combination of methods);
- The rights and responsibilities of the witness, especially as they will affect whether counsel or union representatives will be present.

## *The Physical Environment*

The physical environment in which an interview is conducted can have a tremendous impact on the ability to conduct a successful interview. The physical environment includes not only the interview room itself, but what the witness will, and will not, be permitted to do during the course of the interview, as these physical factors definitely influence mental activity and the control of the interview.

The physical environment such as comfort, noise, privacy, distance between the interviewer and witness, seating arrangement and territoriality affects interviews. You can enhance the witness's concentration and motivation with a well-lighted, pleasantly painted, moderately sized room that has a comfortable temperature and proper ventilation.

Conversely, noise, movement and interruptions, especially telephone calls, disrupt concentration, thought patterns and the mood of the interview. People have difficulty listening and thinking when they see cars on the street outside a window, persons moving about in an outer office, or other investigative personnel coming and going. You must provide privacy and a good atmosphere for an effective interview to take place.

Generally, the person sitting behind a desk, whether the interviewer or witness, gains power and formality. For the majority of interviews planned by the investigator, all communications barriers such as desks, tables, personal items, etc., should be eliminated. The elimination of physical structures limits the ability of the witness to hide behind barriers that can provide a feeling of security as well as emotional and psychological support. For friendly witnesses, the room should be casual and comfortable. For a hostile witness or implicated person, the room should be sparsely furnished with perhaps only chairs for the interview participants.

## *The Number and Roles of Interviewers*

In a potentially provocative interview, two investigators should conduct an interview of a significant witness. There are a number of reasons for following this rule, and when a second trained investigator is not available, another trustworthy person may be used as a stand-in. Using two interviewers allows one to concentrate on asking questions and observing body language, while the other takes notes and reviews the outline to ensure nothing is skipped. The note-taker can also provide periodic summaries mid-interview, and a concluding summary at the end, to ensure accuracy.

Using two interviewers minimizes the likelihood that you and the witness will disagree as to what happened during the interview after it is completed, and make it more likely that any disagreement that does arise will be resolved in your favor.

When two investigators are available, one assumes the role of the primary interviewer and takes the major role in the interview. The primary interviewer makes the introductions, states the purpose, establishes rapport, and asks the first series of questions. The primary interviewer is responsible for setting the tone of the interview, setting the parameters (if any), initiating the interview and observing the witness via all modes of communication. The primary also ensures that secondary interviewers know exactly what is required of them.

The primary and secondary interviewers should not interrupt each other. This allows each investigator to plan his or her own strategy and employ that strategy throughout the interview. The investigators may decide to switch roles as topics change, or at other logical break points. This allows the investigators to display different personalities to the witness, in order to develop the most information from each witness.

## Whom to Interview

A natural temptation is to believe that the more people you speak to, the more complete the investigation will be. Resist the temptation. Interviewing everyone may be a sign that you do not have an investigation strategy.

An investigation is disruptive, so you want to minimize the amount you distract the business group from doing their daily jobs. Also, the more people you speak to, the more likely it is that the information you discuss in the interviews will get shared and circulated, thereby tainting the quality of the information you get later on from other people. Finally, because perceptions and motivations differ from person to person, you risk muddling up your findings with conflicting statements and recollections that you now have to reconcile.

In a workplace investigation, generally plan to interview the following people:
- The reporter (if identified);
- The subject of the investigation;
- Anyone who observed a relevant incident;
- Other witnesses with relevant information, whether identified by the complaining employee or the subject;
- Authors of relevant documents;
- The supervisor of the subject;
- People whom the reporter has asked you to interview;
- People—or at least some of them—whom the subject has asked you to interview. (This is not only to get potentially relevant information. Interviewing these people reinforces the procedural fairness of the process by facilitating the subject's efforts to respond to the allegations.)

Stay focused on the limited scope of the investigation. Seek interviews with those people who have first-hand knowledge of the situation.

---

**Process Pointer:** Pick an "anchor" witness. This person gives you the fullest picture of the investigation facts. You can then use this information as the framework for other witnesses. The others will fill in the facts and bolster the ones you know.

## Where to Conduct the Interview

The place in which the interview occurs affects your effectiveness. A witness who fears that his co-workers may hear what he says or see him speaking to you is not going to give you all the information you might otherwise gather. Conversely, a witness who feels very comfortable and protected in his statements is likely to share more with you than even he may have intended. After all, once people start speaking comfortably, their natural protective defenses begin to drop and the information starts flowing.

The location of the interview should be a neutral place that is conducive to effective information-gathering and protects the fairness of the process. Pursue an interview and not a criminal interrogation. It should be a relatively benign environment, and the witness should be physically free to get up and leave at any time. The room should be at normal temperature and should be free of distractions. Forget the stereotype of the bare room, single chair and spotlight.

Interviews in restaurants or other public places should be only used as a last resort because there are too many distractions and risks to confidentiality. However, they can put a witness at ease because of its public, non-worksite nature. Off-site and home visits can be useful, however, when you need to gain the witness's cooperation to further the objectives of the investigation. Maintaining the secrecy of the interview enables the investigation to remain secret if the witness agrees to cooperate. An off-site location might also be chosen if there is any concern about violence or other disruption in the workplace as a result of confronting the witness.

## Order of Interviews

As a general rule, documents should be examined before interviews begin. This will give you an understanding of the potential evidentiary value of the investigation, as well as to protect the security of documents. It will also allow you to understand the nature of the matters at issue, to identify key players, and to plan for interviews.

Because the investigation has begun, we will assume that you have already interviewed the reporter to determine if probable cause existed to begin the investigation. It is then often best to work with people having the most facts first, then branching out to interview those who can complete the investigation picture by providing supplemental information.

In general, the implicated person is interviewed last. There may be a temptation to confront and/or suspend those suspected of misconduct. However, this must be balanced against the extent to which critical fact-finding will be impeded at an early stage of the investigation. Pre-confrontation investigation will uncover important facts reflecting the nature and extent of the misconduct, allowing the company to assess the actual harm. Facts that directly or circumstantially implicate the investigation subject may also be uncovered. This will enhance the likelihood that the later confrontation will be successful. Also, before the confrontation, the company must consider the legality of certain investigation techniques, the subject's rights and the business implications if the employee is dismissed. Only by carefully considering these issues in advance can you effectively design a strategy for confronting the employee.

Even if you believe that the implicated person will not offer a confession and will likely deny the allegations, an interview is still necessary. Inform the implicated person's immediate supervisor of the report and your intention to interview the individual. Ask the supervisor to be vigilant for further problems, retaliation or other reactions that may affect the investigation. The implicated person should be given full—or as full as reasonably possible—information about the report against him and a full opportunity to explain and defend against the allegations. Reinforce the fairness of the process by giving the implicated person every opportunity to explain his or her actions.

In some circumstances, however, you may need to conduct interviews without advance warning. Surprise interviews may be necessary when there is a concern that witnesses will alter or destroy evidence or that witnesses will confer with each other in an attempt to make their accounts consistent.

If all else fails, begin at the bottom and work up the chain of responsibility rather than begin at the top and work down. Productive sources can always be re-interviewed later to ask follow-up questions.

---

**Process Pointer:** Honest people have little tolerance for theft or serious misconduct. A dishonest person may be more sympathetic when hearing about an incident, speculating that the wrongdoer possibly had a good reason for doing it.

> **Process Pointer:** Keep in mind that employees rarely volunteer information about wrongdoing. Even innocent employees who observed but did not participate in the misconduct will be uncomfortable discussing it. It may be the taboo against "ratting" on others, or it may be a concern that you may consider them a participant as well. But when the right questions are asked, the information will come out. Misconduct is hard to conceal.

### *Collecting Information from Third Parties*

Some investigations include interviews with third parties such as vendors or former employees. Approach these witnesses cautiously. Consider whether a company representative who knows the witness should make the initial contact on your behalf. Be careful to avoid disclosing confidential or fault-related issues to the witness. Remain vigilant to avoid compromising the protections of any applicable legal privileges.

Ideally, third-party witnesses should not be interviewed until after you have obtained as much information as possible from internal sources. This will allow you to disclose only those issues for which the witness becomes a critical source of information. It also reduces the risk that you will be dependent on the third party's cooperation.

### *Interview Dynamics*

Every human interaction has interpersonal dynamics. So do interviews. In an interview, you must gain and continually control the discussion. If you do not control the witness, the witness will likely divert the interview process, leading the interview in directions the witness chooses. Worse, the witness can become the interviewer.

Control simply means the ability to get the witness to respond. Response is the key element. The witness will always respond somehow. The critical issue is whether the witness will respond as you want. Control over the interview is derived from your ability to persuade the witness to respond in the desired manner. An interview should be neither an argument nor a debate.

Never get angry if the witness becomes difficult and frustrating. Becoming angry amounts to giving control of your emotions to the witness, which is the opposite of your goal—to control the witness's emotions. If you cannot control your own emotions, you cannot control the witness. Whatever the implicated person did, he did not do it to you personally. (And if he did, you should not be conducting the investigation.) Recognize the investigation as a business problem that needs to be resolved in a business-like manner.

## *Preparing for the Interview*

Preparing for the interview is essential. The preparation will not only help the investigation. It will convey to the witness that the investigator is thoroughly interested in the matter under investigation.

As a practical matter, try to speak to a witness only once. An interview should be a planned procedure, so each interview involves the development of a plan. The witness—and especially the subject of the investigation—likely anticipates what you will discuss. It is easy to overlook an important issue if interviews are conducted without careful focus on the issues to be addressed.

> **Process Pointer:** Some interviewers make the mistake of not preparing in advance, especially those with plenty of experience. This is wrong. If you are not already sure what you are going to ask the witness, you are more than likely not going to get the information you need. Just jot down the key areas you want to explore.

Carefully consider what questions will be asked and what statements will be made at the start and close of the interview, and how you will document both the information obtained from and the instruction and assurances provided to the witness. Draft in advance an outline of the remarks that will be made in an opening statement, a preliminary list of questions to be asked (but not a script), and a checklist of instructions appropriate to the person being interviewed.

Prepare your outline before each interview. Sometimes you will be able to use the same outline with several witnesses. Nonetheless, review it before interviewing each witness. The exercise of preparing the outline forces you to think through what information this witness is most likely to have and how that information fits into the rest of your investigation. The outline also lets you think about the most effective order of questioning. Don't forget that planning an interview also means that you also consider when you should ask a question. You may get favorable information from a witness more effectively if you ask the easier questions before you ask the ones that are more confrontational.

Be thoroughly familiar with the substance of the investigation. Once the interview begins, an investigator who lacks a working knowledge of the issues involved will have difficulty identifying discrepancies or omissions in the witness's statements. Also, there may be a tendency for an uninformed investigator to look at paper instead of people. Once the interview starts, all new information is going to come from the witness, not the file.

To the extent possible, know everything possible about the witness. He could be a good source of institutional knowledge about the company or the business processes involved. You might want to identify whether he might have some motive that affects his credibility. It may also help you detect if he is evading meaningful responses to issues about which he should know. Moreover, it helps you ensure that, because the interview will be as complete as you can make it, the scope of the investigation remains properly focused on the allegation under investigation.

> **Process Pointer:** If you prepare well, then the witness's information will help you understand the case better and refine your hypothesis. Otherwise, the interview becomes little more than asking questions and writing down the answers. Do the hard work early on, and you won't have to do it later.

### *The Interview Itself*

Most employees you interview will be nervous and understandably apprehensive. You should briefly explain at the start of the interview what is going on and what is expected of the witness.

The introduction to the interview is the hardest part because you have to create the proper impression, enlist the witness's cooperation and explain the nature of your inquiry, all at once.

Read the "Instructions for Witnesses" aloud to the witness. These should be your standard ground rules for the interview. The instructions establish the conventions and assumptions between the parties. These instructions can be found in Appendix K. Be prepared, as a preliminary matter, to answer any questions the witness may have about the interview.

Giving clear interview instructions not only lays the ground rules. It also conveys to the witness that you are in control of the interview and he is not.

The witness should receive a brief explanation of the matter under investigation. Explain why the witness has been included in the investigation (e.g., that he has been identified as someone with a report, has been the subject of misconduct, or has been identified as someone who may have information relevant to the investigation).

There are some introductory questions that you should ask the witness. It is important to know:

- The witness's full name;
- Job title, duties, and times worked;
- Start and end dates of employment;
- Supervisor's name and title;
- The identity of any employees who report directly to the witness;
- Whether the witness has been previously investigated or disciplined;
- What the witness has already been told by others interviewed or involved in the matter;
- What the witness has been told by supervisors or management;
- Whether the witness has been threatened in any way to provide or withhold testimony.

Do not stress time limits on the interview. Do not give the witness the impression that there is a time limit. Enable the witness to believe that the company is sufficiently concerned about the matter. Conversely, do not accept unreasonable limits that would interfere with your ability to conduct a professional interview.

Employees often ask whether they are in trouble or whether they will be disciplined. Be straightforward—it is certainly possible that employees may be disciplined if they committed misconduct, but at this point in the investigation you are just gathering the facts. Never represent to a witness that their cooperation may be offered as a quid pro quo for avoiding any disciplinary, civil or criminal action.

Most interviewers find it helpful to take a break when conducting interviews. The longer or more complex an interview is, the more valuable a break can be. Breaks should probably be taken at least every 90 minutes. It should be taken at a natural spot, not in the middle of the witness's explanations, but usually when you feel that you have obtained almost all the information you need on a particular point.

> **Process Pointer:** Tape recording sounds tempting, but it might have a chilling effect on both you and the witness. Practically speaking, it is also unnecessary. Proper note taking and a timely accurate interview memorandum will sufficiently memorialize the conversation. Similarly, having an administrative person in the room to take notes is a bad idea. The note taker may miss something important or misquote something. Then the notes will be used as proof as to what was or wasn't said. The second problem is that it double-teams the interview, making the witness more uncomfortable.

## *Asking the Best Questions*

Witness interviews are neither pretrial depositions nor courtroom cross-examinations. The purpose of the interview is to elicit truthful and relevant information. Phrase questions and ask them in a manner designed to achieve that purpose. You should never talk down to a witness or use language that the person cannot understand. You should use language that the witness understands, and as the interview proceeds, you should ensure that the witness understands the precise meaning of the words you are using.

> **Process Pointer:** Don't let the witness use legalistic words like "unethical," "assault," "battery," etc. in his responses. The witness may not know the exact meaning—or the implications—of legal terms. You should not use them either, even if you know their precise meaning. The terms could be loaded with emotional baggage that would overwhelm the witness.

Remember the 80:20 rule. You are there to acquire knowledge, not disclose it. The witness should be talking 80 percent of the time, and the investigator only approximately 20 percent of the time. The two most common interviewing errors are (i) the interviewer does not allow the witness to tell his own story, and (ii) the interviewer talks too much.

Focus on the specific misconduct at which the investigation is aimed. Transforming the interview into a wide-ranging inquisition into all possible areas of misconduct is counterproductive because it detracts from the focus of the investigation.

The initial discovery of misconduct may be just a symptom of a much larger problem. Keep alert to that possibility and be prepared to expand your questions accordingly.

Sometimes, managers may want to participate in, or attend, interviews of various witnesses. This can have a chilling effect on the witness. Conduct the interviews of employees without their managers present.

Use a non-confrontational approach. A witness is more likely to cooperate with someone he likes, or at least feels reasonably comfortable with, rather than someone he considers threatening. There may be times when it is necessary to take a more harsh approach. Nonetheless, in the first instance, it is almost always beneficial to try a more disarming approach.

Ask questions in chronological or other systematic order, not randomly. If questioning is confusing, you will lose the witness's train of thought and risk missing information.

Do not expect the witness to have an exact recollection of events that occurred some time ago. It is your obligation to refresh the witness's recollection with documents or other information, if needed.

There are no "magic questions" to ask. But you are better off asking the "who, what, where, when, why and how" questions. However, avoid asking "why" questions until the end. These questions are potentially provocative because they sound moralistic.

Ask open-ended questions. Open-ended questions are more likely to result in your learning what the witness knows. "Who was there?" "What was said?" "Why did you do that?" Open-ended questions encourage the witness to respond. They allow you to learn about the subject, based on how the witness describes himself. They also help the witness relax.

Do not ask close-ended questions. This type of question tends to require a "yes" or "no," or a brief statement at most. These questions do not provide for extended responses and, as a rule, will not allow the witness to relax. The witness is more likely to provide the answer and then stop talking.

Ask straightforward questions. Do not be cute, tricky or shrewd. Your goal is to get information in the simplest, clearest way possible.

The basis of the witness's knowledge is always important. Determine whether the witness is speaking from personal knowledge or just relying on the hearsay statements of others. "How do you know that?" is a question to ask often.

Ask the witness to list all individuals who have knowledge of any of the events. "Who else might know?" is a question to ask often.

Distinguish between words used by the witness and situations where the witness simply agrees with a question or statement. Consider the wording of leading questions and whose words were used. Identify situations where there were only agreements with statements you made or the witness made the actual statements. Allow the witness to reject your characterization if he doesn't accept it. You want the most accurate recollections possible.

The investigation should identify any mitigating circumstances that may affect the assessment of fault, such as personal or health problems.

It may not always be possible, but try to structure questions in a way that does not call attention to particular problem areas. The order of questions as well as your demeanor in asking them can alert a witness to the focus and severity of the problem being investigated. If there is something you would prefer to remain highly confidential, take care in structuring and asking the questions about it. (Some experienced investigators even include subjects of no real relevance to avoid tipping the witness off to the nature of the inquiry.)

Save unfriendly or embarrassing questions until the end of the interview. Beginning with the "tough" questions may cause the witness to become defensive.

On key factual areas, it can be valuable to return to the same question more than once in different ways. People often remember things in waves, and this approach may develop additional detail.

If a person does not remember, try to help by asking questions that help recreate the situation when the event occurred, but do not suggest an answer.

Empathy is important. This is the feeling associated with emotional identification with another person. When used correctly, this mutual concern encourages the free flow of information. Take a non-judgmental attitude, and be careful to disguise any negative feelings or lack of compassion for the witness.

Silence is a great technique. Many people cannot stand silence and find this unnerving. They will fill up the void with talk, often saying something they had no intention of revealing. The average person expects no more than seven seconds of silence during a conversation. If you don't say anything after the witness answers a question, the witness will frequently give you more information than he intended to give you. The silence effectively pressures the subject into offering more information by communicating that you feel that the answer was not complete. Silence can also be an effective way to undermine a witness who is cocky and confident in his or her own ability to control the discussion. The witness, and not you, should become uncomfortable with the silence.

Avoid doing anything that might be taken as an attempt to influence the witness's answers. Avoid characterizing the company's position, summarizing the statements of other witnesses, or selectively presenting documents in a way that may distort the facts. Misleading a witness, even unintentionally, undermines the value of his information.

There is always the possibility that the information the witness is providing contradicts either something he said earlier or a piece of information gathered from another source. One of the most effective techniques is to note the contradictions and then, at the appropriate point, ask the witness how these contradictory facts could be true (or reconciled). Recall them individually and review the facts again.

Ask again at the end of the interview: "Is there anything else relevant to this matter that I should know? Is there anything I missed? What else should I ask you? What other documents are important? Who else knows about this? Who else can help me with this information? Is there a question I should have asked and didn't? Is there anything else you know about this?" Ask several of these questions. It is very important to document these questions to support the fact that the witness was asked for all relevant information.

---

**Process Pointer:** Don't write your questions in advance. You will lock yourself into only the points your questions cover. If the witness discusses something interesting that is not in your script, you will likely ignore it. Also, a script will make you more concerned about your questions rather than the witness's answers.

Take your time. If you finish the interview but think you did not get all the facts you could have, you likely rushed through it.

## Facilitators of communication

Facilitators of communication are the forces that make conversations easier to accomplish. These dynamics play a role in every conversation, including a risk-assessment interview. There are six common facilitators:

- **Fulfilling expectations.** When people communicate, they communicate their expectations of what they want the other person to do. (Nodding your head in agreement is one such way.) The interviewer communicates his expectations to the employee, such as an expectation of cooperation and truth-telling.
- **Recognition.** Everyone needs the recognition and esteem of others. People "perform" in exchange for recognition and other social rewards. Interviewers who acknowledge the contributions of the employees will get better results.
- **Altruistic appeals.** People need to identify with a higher value besides self interest. Altruistic feelings increase a person's self-esteem through association.
- **Sympathetic understanding.** People need the sympathy of others and to share their joys, fears, successes and failures. This is not recognition for esteem as much as a common humanity. Empathy leads to an emotional identification with another person. When used correctly, the mutual concern facilitates the free flow of information.
- **Catharsis.** This is a release from unpleasant emotional tensions. People feel better talking about something that bothers them.
- **Extrinsic rewards.** An employee may be motivated by more than a desire to be helpful to the investigation. The reward could be money, privileges or prestige.

Just as some dynamics facilitate communication, some factors inhibit it:

- **Ego threat.** This dynamic actually has three parts.
  - **Repression** – Employees who have done the wrong thing may be denying it to themselves too. They may have subconsciously forgotten it. (This happens with embezzlers when they repress what they did because it conflicts with their moral code.)
  - **Disapproval.** An employee may have information but may not want to tell you because he feels that you will condemn him.
  - **Loss of status.** An employee may fear a loss of status if the information comes out.

- **Etiquette.** Some answers would be considered in poor taste or things that are not discussed in front of women. The interviewer can address this factor by anticipating the setting for the interview.
- **Trauma.** This is an acutely unpleasant feeling associated with reporting the experience.
- **Forgetting.** This is a frequent obstacle. It can be related to the original emotional impact of the event and the degree it relates to a person's ego. Another factor is the time that has elapsed. Another factor is the nature of the interview setting.

> **Process Pointer:** Don't overlook the possibility that a witness's resistance may be based on a fear of retaliation. If the witness does not want to "rat" on a friend, instruct the witness that you are just a fact gatherer trying to learn as much as you can. Remind him that someone else is the judge and jury.

### Having the Gall to Ask

Investigations require you to ask uncomfortable questions to witnesses. Unfortunately, this is unavoidable, and investigators should embrace this reality.

In many investigations, the issues you are investigating are provocative. Someone may be fired. Someone may not want to implicate another person. Someone may have done something terrible. But you have to know about it.

It is a normal human reaction to want to avoid asking tough or embarrassing questions. It takes a certain amount of gall to ask someone if he stole money, if he sent erotic messages to a co-worker, if he forged company records. But conducting a proper investigation requires you to be brave enough to ask questions that would be rude and intrusive in other situations. To justify asking the questions, the participants should agree before you ask them that these questions are necessary for the investigation.

Do not be reluctant to make the person uncomfortable. It is your job to find out the truth and make it hard for anyone to tell you anything less.

## *The Written Statement*

Statements play an important role in investigations. If the witness has been handled right, the witness may not likely object to offering a written statement.

Invite the witness to submit a written personal statement of the relevant facts. (This is included in the witness instructions, and a template form may be found in Appendix L.) This statement is not the same as a voluntary statement furnished by someone making a confession. This statement is intended to reinforce the procedural fairness of the investigation. The statement should contain a record of the issues raised, the witness's version of what happened, who was involved, witnesses, dates, etc. The statement should also respond to or explain any evidence. Your questions necessarily reflect those matters about which you want information. The witness statement, by contrast, reflects what the witness wants to say about the matter. The written statement may give you additional information about the investigation. The written statement should be signed, dated and added to the investigation file.

## *Closing the Interview*

The interview should be closed on a positive note. Use this opportunity to review key facts elicited during the interview to be certain these points were correctly understood.

At the end of the interview, thank the witness for the information furnished. Give the witness your telephone number or email address if more information becomes available or is remembered. Keep the door open for future contact if he would like to add or change anything. The goal is to obtain the most accurate information possible. An interview is not intended to be a memory test.

If you asked the witness to furnish documents, renew that request and agree to a list and date for production, if possible, of the needed documents. Consider giving the witness a written list confirming the items he has to furnish.

Tell the witness that appropriate management personnel will make any final determination regarding the best way to resolve the issue, but stress that the witness's input is valuable and will be considered seriously. The witness should be told that the results of the investigation remain confidential, and that the specific corrective actions may not be communicated to the witness.

The interview does not need to cover every conceivable fact, event and conduct. All you need to move forward are the material facts concerning the subject matter of the investigation.

> **Process Pointer:** Retain goodwill. In closing the interview, take the time to preserve the rapport with the witness. You may need to contact him again. He can also become an advocate of your investigation process.
>
> Stay alert to communications inhibitors such as time demands, threats to the witness's ego, trauma and memory lapses. Be prepared to navigate around them.
>
> Remember the things that facilitate communication: recognition, altruistic appeals, sympathy and catharsis. Use these to keep the information flowing.

## G) Telephone Interviews

### Differences

The obvious difference between face-to-face interviews and telephone interviews is that you cannot see the person you are interviewing. In some cases, you cannot be sure you are talking to the person you are attempting to interview. Therefore, in the absence of other verification, you must be careful to ask questions that would ensure a reasonable belief that the people you are talking to are the people they claim to be.

### Problems with Telephone Interviews

In a telephone interview, people do not truly communicate. Therefore, you need to be an "active listener" to obtain all the information that is being passed over the telephone. Although the telephone interview allows the speakers to gather and/or exchange facts, information and ideas, the inability to read the nonverbal aspect of the message complicates the process and makes thorough evaluation of the witness and the information provided difficult.

Telephone interviews should be avoided where possible, especially in the case of implicated people and important witnesses. Reporter interviews done in-person are also preferred, but this is not always possible because many complaints come via the telephone hotline and provide no means of follow-up. It is also recognized that cost becomes a factor when in-person interviews require travel expenses. Effective time management may also be a factor.

Try to limit telephone interviews to instances where they will have less impact—for witnesses who only provide background information, for use as a follow-up technique after the primary interview has been conducted in-person, and for use as a preliminary inquiry technique to determine the extent of someone's knowledge or develop leads.

### *Telephone Interview Guidelines*

The guidelines for telephone interviews are similar to face-to-face interviews with a few additions and a slightly different emphasis on others. Consider the following:

- Asking a second interviewer to be present in the room and take notes;
- Getting call-back numbers and setting up a time for continuation, if necessary, at the start of the phone conversation in case one of you has to end the call before the interview is completed;
- Reviewing notes with the witness more frequently during the interview to ensure that if the interview is terminated prematurely, the information obtained to that point is accurate;
- Using video conferencing equipment when available in order to obtain more of the nonverbal communications that would be available in an in-person interview. Although more expensive than a phone call, it is usually less expensive than the cost of flying or driving to a distant location.

### *Interview Techniques*

The techniques are much the same as the face-to-face interview, but take on more importance because of the quality of response needed. For example, open-ended questions allow for a long narrative response and are very good during an in-person interview, but less useful in a telephone interview due to your inability to perceive the nonverbal aspect of the communication. Also, a narrative telephone response may require interruptions that may destroy continuity and could appear to be rude if the witness drifts off the subject.

Probing questions are designed to get underlying reasons for previous comments. They are useful when trying to get the witness to focus on certain aspects of the topic(s) on which you want further information. Direct questions are a good method to narrow the range of answers geared toward gathering specific information about a specific topic.

Leading questions are phrased in such a way that the witness thinks there is an expected or appropriate response. This type of question can create a climate in which the witness becomes defensive and feels manipulated. It can be useful in getting the witness focused when he is vague or speaking in generalities. Question-softening techniques are very useful during telephone interviews. Begin questions with the words "I am curious....?" or "I was wondering....?" or "Would you happen to know....?"

Keep your focus on the interview. During a telephone interview, you will likely be sitting at your desk, tempted to check emails or surf the internet to keep your eyes busy. This will, of course, distract you from the urgency to listen carefully. Instead, put yourself into the same mental zone as if you were physically in the room.

Don't be in a hurry to end a telephone interview. Much information may be relayed in small talk and casual conversation when the witness thinks the interview is over. Review investigative notes with the witness to ensure agreement as to what the issues are and what was said about them. If you didn't complete the interview in the time available, make an appointment and get the telephone number to talk to the person again to obtain the information. If appropriate, witnesses may volunteer or be asked to provide documents to support their complaints or to corroborate information. If they are making a report of actual or suspected misconduct, it is reasonable to expect them to provide the information to support the report, and they should be told so. Avoid putting pressure on witnesses during a telephone interview because they could become hostile, lose rapport, and hang up.

## H) Interviewing the Implicated Employee

A proper workplace investigations process provides the implicated person with an opportunity to respond to the allegations. When you properly interview the implicated person, you fulfill any fundamental-fairness rights that he might enjoy, and if he admits to wrongdoing, that statement can be used as proof of guilt.

## *The Right to Respond*

The implicated person should be reasonably provided with an opportunity to respond to the allegation and the information developed against him. If the implicated person denies the allegation, he should be offered the opportunity to assist in the investigation to establish his innocence. Even if the weight of the information uncovered tends to substantiate the allegation, the investigation is not over until the implicated person is allowed the opportunity to offer some facts to support his innocence.

Admissions are your strongest proof in an investigation because, of course, the statements come directly from the implicated person. It also provides some comfort to the investigator because it frees the investigator from having to draw conclusions about guilt from the available facts. In many investigations, there will be little disagreement about the facts, and the difference between guilt or innocence will depend on the interpretation of what those facts mean—was the boss's request for a date simple flirting or an attempt for a forbidden quid pro quo for that promotion? The admission, for example, that the implicated person knew his actions violated company policy when he did them can be very helpful.

## *Interrogating the Implicated Person*

There is a fundamental difference between an interview and an interrogation. The dynamics of the two are completely opposite.

An interview is a non-accusatory fact gathering conversation to determine facts, sequences of events, alibis, or to confirm information with a specific witness. The questions are generally open-ended, and the witness does most of the talking. If close-ended questions are asked, the investigator is usually trying to clearly establish certain facts or to confirm important details. The investigator is not looking for a confession but only for the witness to confirm or deny specific pieces of information.

An interrogation is fundamentally different. It is conducted when the investigator has a valid basis to believe that the implicated person actually committed some wrongdoing. It is a search for admissions and a confession, and these will independently confirm the investigation findings.

There is a difference between an admission and a confession. In most investigations, you seek the former. A confession, in our context, is essentially a blanket statement that the implicated person committed misconduct. An admission is the implicated person's acknowledgement that he committed certain material acts. For example, "yes, I stole the money" is a confession. Admissions, in contrast, would be: he took the money, he did not have permission to take it, he knew he was violating company policy when he did, his boss did not know, he had no intention to pay the money back, and he forged his boss's signature on the form.

The admission or confession will also establish the person's participation in the wrongdoing. You are looking for information that establishes the implicated person's culpability and mental state, which are relevant to identifying mitigating circumstance. This information also helps identify weaknesses in internal controls. This information is also relevant later when management determines post-investigation steps like disciplinary action.

## *Preparing for the Interrogation*

An interview of the implicated person must be planned carefully. The purpose of this session is to learn the truth and obtain admissions of material facts. Remember that you are not looking to gather objective information any more, other than an explanation of his conduct or an offer of mitigating facts. The implicated person is unlikely to give you additional facts that you can reasonably use (unless the implicated person leads you to some new avenue of inquiry).

> **Process Pointer:** In a confrontational interview, keep co-workers and managers outside the room. It is difficult for any implicated person to confess in front of friends or colleagues.
>
> If you think someone else worked with the implicated person in committing the wrongdoing, interview that other person first. This will give you more evidence with which to confront the implicated person.
>
> Before you confront the implicated person, have your documents and statements of others handy to prove up your allegation.

> **Process Pointer:** Theme development makes a confession more palatable. The implicated person may have a moral—though not legal—justification for what he did. Morally acceptable themes like financial duress, an intention to pay the money back, poor employer treatment, etc. make it easier for an implicated person to confess.

As you prepare for the interrogation, consider the implicated person's possible motives for committing the wrongdoing. Did he do it for the money? To save his job? To impress someone? When you have some idea—even if it is only a working hypothesis—you can then focus the interview in that direction.

The theme of this interview should include some explanation as to why an investigation was conducted and what leads you to believe that the person committed the misconduct. It is not necessary to make accusations—in fact, it will probably chill the conversation—but you need the implicated person to understand that you are there for a reason and your interview is not just a "fishing expedition."

You should also clearly state that you are only investigating the allegation and that you have no control over post-investigative steps. This will avoid any claim later on that the implicated person admitted fault only because you said that it would save his job.

> **Process Pointer:** Resist the temptation to bully someone to give you an admission or confession. You will more likely achieve your result if you are friendly and cooperative. People who feel they are being attacked will defensively resist. Get the witness relaxed and talking and see what happens.
>
> Develop the information from the witness before confronting him with any wrongdoing you suspect. Once you confront the witness, you have restricted the flow of facts you are capable of getting.
>
> Remember there is no Fifth Amendment privilege. Employees have no real right to refuse to cooperate and assist the investigation. Also, if an implicated employee claims to be innocent, ask him to point out the proof that shows that. It may speed up your investigations process.

> **Process Pointer:** When seeking an admission, you have to be reasonably convinced that the implicated person did the act. You want your interview to distinguish an innocent person from a guilty one. If your goal is to obtain information, then do not use interrogation-style questioning.

### Dos and Don'ts of Interrogations

The following is a list of dos and don'ts that can be helpful to the investigator:

- Do use silence as a weapon—ask a direct question and wait for a response;
- Do keep questions short;
- Do ask only one question at a time;
- Do question the answers you get;
- Do guard yourself against giving away information;
- Don't make promises of any kind;
- Don't lose your patience or persistence;
- Don't threaten the implicated employee;
- Don't show surprise at any answers;
- Don't use profanity or lower yourself to the level of others;
- Don't lie. Whatever you tell must be the truth;
- Don't ever lose your temper—this turns over control to the implicated person, and you will lose the interrogation;
- Don't make excuses for the implicated person. If you do and it shows up in your documentation, those excuses are likely to be used by the employee for his benefit. Let him make his own excuses;
- The person being interrogated may be psychologically and emotionally suffering because of your questions. Many wrongdoers want to confess their misconduct or at least try to explain what they were doing. Help them do that.

## l) Detecting Insincerity

It is human nature to resist doing something uncomfortable. Admitting your wrongdoing and putting your job at risk is one of those things. The more significant the misconduct, the more an implicated person will be tempted to deny it or somehow explain it away. He may also try to distance himself psychologically from the situation.

A key component of the interview process is determining the witness's credibility and the weight to be given to the information offered. When you assess credibility, you may detect a deception.

To assess credibility, ask yourself the following questions:

- Was the witness physically present and aware of what was happening during the incident?
- How well developed are the witness's powers of observation?
- Is what the witness telling you logical? Does it make sense? Truthful stories are logical. They do not appear to be scripted. Truthful statements are detailed in their presentation of the setting of an event. They reproduce some of the actual conversations, character and mannerisms of the key players in the story.
- What was the witness's demeanor?
- Did the witness make contradictory statements?
- Did the witness have a reason to lie?
- Does the witness have any known or suspected bias?
- Does the witness stand to gain from any particular outcome?
- What are the witness's relationships to other witnesses and the subject of the investigation?

Also look for the following verbal indicators of deception:

- Attempts to evade questions;
- Vague answers;
- Conflicting information;
- Different answers to the same or similar questions;
- Patently inaccurate information.

The way in which our bodies show that we are attempting to deceive is referred to as "nonverbal leakage." These are a series of body language clues that indicate insincerity.

An estimated 70 percent of communication is non-verbal. Carefully observe the witness's body posture and physical activity. Everyone uses body language to express themselves. Watch for changes in appearance in response to certain questions. Most people under stress are unaware of their reactions. Use these observations when formulating questions. Look for the following physical indicators of deception:

- **Grooming gestures.** This includes rubbing the hands together, biting fingernails, tapping, swinging, arching the feet, and picking lint or pulling threads off clothes.

- **Eye contact.** Avoiding eye contact conveys nervousness and a lack of confidence.
- **Distance.** Someone who is lying will try to move away from you in order to put more space between you.
- **Behavior.** Appearing tense, disturbed, excited or agitated.

These manifestations of nervousness may or may not indicate the presence of deception. Don't base your conclusions on the observation of just one indicator. Watch for clusters of symptoms, noting where they occur in the interview.

Even an innocent person will feel and exhibit some degree of nervousness in the interview. Look for changes of physical response beyond those manifestations of nervousness the witness displayed when the interview began.

Begin with the presumption that the witness is telling the truth. To begin the interview with a predetermined belief that the witness will be lying is counterproductive. It will likely influence the witness's responses.

Your goal is to obtain as much accurate information as possible. But even false information is useful if you know it is false. It may be easier to terminate an employee for lying during an investigation than it is to prove that they actually committed the misconduct under investigation.

Accept that nearly everyone you interview has his or own agenda or set of objectives (shifting blame, promoting their own interests, or shading the facts in a favorable way, for example). In most instances, it is not hard to see what they are trying to do, and you can discount their information accordingly. In other cases, a process of triangulation will be necessary to tighten down on the true factual picture.

---

**Process Pointer:** People lie if they believe that lying helps them more than telling you the truth. You need to convince the witness that telling the truth is better for him than lying through the interview.

Lying is not a natural human behavior. It has to be done consciously. Consequently, it can be observed. But don't jump to conclusions about the reasons the witness may be lying. Liars have plenty of reasons for what they do.

Truthfulness is signaled by an acute memory, a perceptive recounting of facts, and a flowing narration. Truthful witnesses display a consistent recollection of details and attempt to explain related specifics, often offering more information than they were asked for. They allow the investigator to see their mental wheels turn in search of additional details. They are open and relaxed in their manner of speech, though they may be nervous about the interview. They clearly explain what happened, and they want to be correct.

Deception, by contrast, is the intentional act of concealing or distorting the truth for the purpose of misleading. Witnesses deceive when they deliberately hide from the interviewer what they saw or did, and why they did it.

## *Types of Lies*

During an interview, the witness may engage in a variety of different attempts to deceive you. There are five basic types of lies that the witness may use.

The first type of lie is the simple denial. Its simplicity might lead you to think that this type would be chosen often. But many people don't deny misconduct directly. Psychologists call this "cognitive dissonance." To avoid this, a witness will go to great lengths to avoid having to deny it directly.

The second type of lie is the lie of omission. This is the most common type. It is also the simplest lie because the witness tells the truth but leaves out the information that could be embarrassing or incriminating. Because the remaining part of the witness's statement is true, it can be repeated consistently. If the witness is presented with the omitted information, he can just respond that he forgot to mention it. A lie of omission can succeed if you are not prepared to force the subject by mentioning the excluded information.

The third type is the lie of fabrication. This is the most difficult type of lie because it requires the witness to be inventive and have a good memory to keep the lie consistent. This type of lie also creates the most stress for the witness.

Ask questions when a lie of fabrication is suspected, to show that the explanation does not hold up to specific questioning. If the investigation can disprove the witness's sequence of events or details, that result may prove as significant as a confession of wrongdoing.

The fourth type of lie is minimization. Here, the witness offers a small admission of fault hoping that you will be satisfied and discontinue any further questioning. When this type of lie is used, it is a strong indication that additional information is being withheld.

The final type of lie is the lie of exaggeration. A witness may exaggerate the actions of another person or an aspect of a particular conversation. The lie may be used by someone who wants to increase the value of his information or inflate his own importance. If you maintain a healthy skepticism and question each claim, you should be able to identify any exaggerations.

Lies told in an interview can be as powerful as a confession. Lying in a workplace investigation likely exposes the employee to disciplinary action. An investigator must constantly be aware of the possibility that the subject is withholding information or intentionally attempting to deceive.

## J) Common Interview Problems

Good interviewers use a great variety of their personal traits, but must be able to adjust their personal styles to harmonize with the traits and moods of the witness. There are many errors that you can make while doing this. Some of the most significant are:

- **Showing personal prejudice or allowing prejudice to influence the conduct of the interview** destroys your objectivity and credibility, becoming a self-fulfilling prophecy;
- **Lying** destroys your credibility and encourages similar behavior from the witness;
- **Hurrying** encourages mistakes and omissions and leads to your improperly evaluating the veracity of the information provided;
- **Making assumptions, drawing unconfirmed inferences, jumping to conclusions** may result in important information not being requested or allowing false or unverifiable information to be introduced into the investigation;
- **Making promises you can't keep.** This destroys the investigator's credibility and reputation, and may cause the witness to react negatively to other investigative personnel in the future;
- **Looking down at or degrading the witness, showing a contemptuous attitude** may anger witnesses and encourage unnecessary emotional barriers;

- **Placing too much value on minor inconsistencies** allows you and the interview to get "hung up" on minor or irrelevant issues;
- **Bluffing** destroys the interviewer's credibility and may allow the witness to take charge of the interview;
- **Anger** results in control of the session reverting to the witness; it serves as a relief to the witness and is a distraction from the information gathering process;
- **Underestimating the mental abilities of witnesses, especially by talking down to them** antagonizes witnesses and invites them to trip up the investigator.

## *Questioning Techniques to Avoid*

Avoid leading questions during free narrative and direct examination. They tend to cause witnesses to give the answer they think you want to hear, rather than what they know to be the truth.

A common investigator error is the use of negatively phrased questions. The question that is phrased in the negative appears to be a rather serious problem, even among very experienced investigators. The negatively phrased question not only suggests that the response is to be "no," but also states that no is the right answer. For example, the question, "You wouldn't do that, would you?" clearly implies you expect a negative response. Most negatively phrased questions are also leading.

Compound questions are questions asked in rapid succession before the witness can respond to the first question. This includes rephrasing the original question and may include "either or" questions. This method of questioning should be avoided because, at best, it confuses the witness and, at worst, can cause information to be missed or overlooked. Compound questions tend to show a lack of experience and may indicate when you are excited, tense or lost.

When faced with multiple questions, witnesses are likely to answer only the question or questions they remember or that are the least threatening to them. The answers to the other questions are most often lost. For the implicated person, compound questions offer an out because he may answer only the least incriminating questions and those that create the least amount of stress. Compound questions allow the implicated person to conceal information while appearing to be forthcoming and cooperative. Complex questions are complicated, not easily understood and cover more than one topic. Complex questions tend to confuse the witness and lead to an "I don't know" or an unintended false answer.

### *Requesting a Lawyer*

A witness may ask if he needs a lawyer. This poses a problem that requires an immediate response. While everyone has the right to consult an attorney, your company has the right to require its employees to disclose information that they have that related to the company's business. The conventional wisdom is to reply that only the witness should make that decision. Offer no opinion on whether the witness needs a lawyer. If you are an attorney, repeat that you are representing the company and cannot provide the witness with any legal advice. Your notes should state the substance of this exchange during the interview. Management is not required to allow interview subjects to have a lawyer and can insist that the interview continue with the witness without a lawyer present. The company is entitled to one-on-one communications with its employees, and not ones filtered through attorneys or made more difficult by the legal adversary process.

Sometimes you may choose to allow the witness to bring an attorney. This usually happens when you want the witness's information more than you want to fight about a lawyer being present. If so, you must not let the attorney take over the interview or disrupt it in any way. Instead, give him a full opportunity at the end of the interview to state his position.

> **Process Pointer:** Although an employer can fire someone who refuses to cooperate with the investigation, a termination is not going to get you the information you need. Consider the reasons why the person is reluctant to speak with you and see if those concerns can be accommodated. If the employee outright refuses, then develop another investigative strategy. The strategy should consider whether the employee has guilty knowledge that he is trying to keep from you.

### *Placing Conditions on the Interview*

An employee may also insist that an interview take place under certain conditions. These conditions might include (i) the participation of the employee's lawyer; (ii) the tape-recording of the interview; (iii) that certain topics will not be discussed; or (iv) that the company will not disclose certain parts of the interview without that employee's prior consent. This situation requires both you and management to weigh the need for the information against the burdens imposed if the company agrees. If the company agrees, the agreement should be in writing. The company should also consider the extent to which applicable legal privileges against disclosure might be deemed to be waived.

At the beginning of an investigation and at various points during its course, you should make a good-faith assessment whether the matter under investigation poses the risk of criminal liability for the company or any of the employees. If so, you should inform the witness of the option to retain personal counsel and have the personal counsel present during the interview. If requested, be prepared to postpone or suspend the interview long enough to permit the witness to obtain counsel or consider whether to do so.

### *Requests to Have Other People Attend*

In most cases, it is not appropriate to allow witnesses to have friends or relatives present during the interview, because this tends to inhibit candor and full disclosure. You may permit third parties to be present if it appears this would facilitate communications during the interview. The interview record should reflect the presence of third parties. As an alternative, suggest the friend be available in a nearby room.

### *Refusal to Submit to an Interview*

The employees must answer all questions relating to an investigation. An employee may state that he does not want to be interviewed. This problem should be addressed earlier as a matter of company policy. Your company should articulate to its employees that the company has a "talk or walk" policy, meaning that employees must cooperate with a workplace investigation or risk losing their jobs.

While it is generally true that an employee has a duty to cooperate with the investigation, you must never appear to bully the employee into agreeing to the interview. If the interview is essential, your company may very well conclude that it is appropriate to bring disciplinary proceedings against the employee for refusing to cooperate with the investigation.

Employees may have a Fifth Amendment right under the U.S. Constitution not to make self-incriminating statements to the government. They have no equivalent right to refuse to make a statement to their employer, and certainly no constitutional right to keep a job with the company after refusing to talk with company representatives.

However, as with any employee termination related to the investigation, the company should determine, before terminating an employee for not cooperating with the investigation, whether that termination would harm the company's own interests. After all, an employee cannot be expected to cooperate with the company's investigation after being terminated.

### *False Testimony*

Witnesses who knowingly make false statements may be subject to termination. If you believe this may be happening, provide a warning that advises of the penalties for false statements. Witnesses should be advised they are subject to disciplinary action for false statements, which in many cases is an effective warning.

### *Request for Advice*

Sometimes a witness may ask you for advice. You should decline to provide such advice except as it relates to his rights and duties in connection with the investigation, or the procedures relating to the interview. For example, when a witness asks if he may consult with an attorney prior to the interview, it is appropriate to advise that he may do so. However, if a witness then asks whether consultation would be appropriate in this case, you should decline to answer that question.

> **Process Pointer:** When witnesses become difficult with you, resist the temptation to strong-arm their participation. The success of your interview depends on his willingness to give you information. Don't react to witnesses' statements and try to disarm them. Change your approach. And remember that witnesses resist for a variety of reasons and not just to conceal misconduct.

## K) The Interview Memo

If you are going to rely on any of the information from the interview, you must memorialize the witness's statements. Just as a relevant document taken from a filing cabinet serves as a component for your findings, so should a memorandum of the interview. When prepared correctly, it stands as a separate piece of investigation evidence.

> **Process Pointer:** A good memo can protect you later on if the witness denies something or accuses you of an improper line of questioning. Get in the habit of writing complete memos that can stand on their own.

Resist the temptation to simply drop your handwritten notes in the file. Your notes are your subjective understanding of the matters discussed. It will also be written in your unique shorthand. The risk is that others may review these notes and draw different conclusions from your notes. Worse, you may be asked to recall things that happened and not be able to decipher what you wrote. If another person is taking notes, then the risks are compounded, especially the risk that the two sets of notes contradict each other in some way. Either way, your investigation is, practically speaking, deprived of the precise information the witness offered. You have inadvertently inserted yourself into the investigation process by now having to act as some kind of interpreter to explain what the witness said. Stated another way, the value of this witness now depends not on what he said, but rather on what you recall that he said. You are, essentially, now the witness to hearsay information.

Instead, as soon as possible after the interview is completed, draft a simple memo to the file transcribing your notes into simple declarative sentences or a narrative of the conversation. Use as many direct quotes as possible. Then destroy your handwritten notes. The memo should be the sole written recollection of the interview. Through this process, you will identify any gaps in your questioning that will require you to get supplemental information from the witness. You are also more likely to remember details that you left out of your notes but should be added to the memo. If for some reason you cannot decipher your notes, you will then be able to expeditiously correct the situation.

Some propose that the witness should review the memo or sign it to signify that they agree to its accuracy. This should not be done. The memo represents your recording of information gathered from the witness. It does not represent your collaborative process with the witness. The information, if properly gathered, stands on its own even without the agreement of the witness because, presumably, he said those words. There is also a practical problem with soliciting the agreement of the witness. What will you do if the witness disagrees—as opposed to supplementing or clarifying a statement—that he said something that you recalled? How will you reconcile the disagreement? The practical effect of the disagreement will be to undermine the value of that memo by your self-defeating attempt to underscore the fairness of the process.

One word of caution: make the memo a good one. If there is a lawsuit, a complaint to a regulatory agency or even an internal inquiry, the memo is going to be produced. If the witness is key to your investigation findings, any scrutiny of your conclusions will include a scrutiny of that memo. Remember that the memo can be both a sword and a shield. A properly documented interview memo not only will justify a management decision but it can also protect you from a claim that the findings were unsupported or the implicated employee did not admit what he actually admitted to you. It can also prove a negative. For example, if a witness falsely claims that he said something in the interview that somehow favors his position, its omission from a proper, contemporaneously prepared interview memo is going to show that it is more likely than not that the statement was not made.

> **Process Pointer:** Do not write your interview memo in question-and-answer format. It makes reading it tedious, and you could be challenged as to why you asked a particular question and not another.
>
> The interview memo is the heart of the investigation report. Always write a separate one for each witness.
>
> The interview memo should have clear and concise evidence. Write like you speak. Avoid using the third person to describe the interviewer. And don't use stilted or pretentious wording.

## L) Collection and Review of Documents

Documents are an important part of most investigations. Documents frequently identify information that helps prove the wrongdoing. Important information can be found in a variety of document types, including computer records, internal memos, transactional documents, financial records, expense account reports and phone logs.

Documents provide a credible record of the conduct under investigation. Documents generally fall into two categories: paper and electronic. You generally take the lead in document gathering and examination. The process must be thorough and well documented.

Witnesses may be reluctant to supply information voluntarily, especially when it may implicate their own actions or the actions of those they supervise or with whom they work. Similarly, witness recollections of events often fade with time and may be inconsistent with recollections of other witnesses. Documents are essential in the process of refreshing a witness's memory and might also help the investigator reconcile conflicting recollections. Documents can also help determine or assess a person's intent or motive in doing something. Documents often provide the best record of the conduct at issue.

E-mails are especially useful. Instantaneous screen edits and a "point, click, send" culture have eliminated the time delay that used to allow cooler heads to prevail when sending intemperate notes. The prevalence of electronic messages has created a false sense of security in many employees and lulled them into making exchanges of information that they never would do face-to-face. Consequently, an e-mail message may give you valuable insight into the real dynamics that were going on at that moment in time, rather than the careful descriptions of events you might hear in an interview.

Use care to identify relevant documents. The search should also include informal as well as formal company records. In many companies, for example, employees maintain their own personal desk files in addition to the official company files. These need to be included in the search.

But don't overdo it either. An investigation differs from litigation, where lawyers seek every possible shred of paper. You want only the relevant documents. Your goal is to substantiate an allegation of actual or suspected wrongdoing.

The files of potential wrongdoers should be reviewed and all documents appropriate to a particular investigation should be examined, including such items as calendars, letters, e-mails, voicemail messages, expense reports, etc. If there is a concern that an employee may try to hide or destroy files, consider obtaining them without first requesting them from the employee, and perhaps without the employee's knowledge.

The gathering of electronic documents, including e-mails, information stored on networks, diskettes, back-up tapes and personal computers, requires special attention. Best practices for the handling of electronic evidence change constantly. Computers frequently contain smoking-gun evidence.

When needed, meet with appropriate information technology personnel to ensure that all potentially relevant sources have been searched. You will need to know (i) the type and model of the computer used, (ii) the capacity of the internal hard disk and the external disk drives; (iii) the operating system; (iv) the applications used on the computer and where they are stored, and (v) the computer literacy of the implicated person. Electronic document searches frequently result in the recovery of too much data. Using selective word searches, you can filter large amounts of records and data into manageable amounts.

When handling investigation documents, use appropriate precautions. Documents should be indexed so they can be found when needed. Original documents should not be marked or altered in any way. There may be multiple copies of some documents. Retain these copies, especially if they include important margin notes or other markings. It may become important to know which individuals maintained a copy in their files. Compare versions of what appears to be the same document for alterations.

An original document is anything you received from someone else, even if it is a copy. It does not include any copies you made. If you need a working copy of the document, copy the original. Put the original in the file, and mark the copies up as needed. Following this practice will prevent an inadvertent alteration of original documents and ensure that these documents will not be invalidated or challenged later as a result of the your markings.

The authenticity of documents becomes critical in investigations where document tampering is suspected. Therefore, in some instances it may become necessary to obtain the same documents from more than one independent source. Indicate which copy of the document came from which source.

Once documents are obtained, treat the file as confidential and store it in a locked cabinet. Only those persons with a need to know should be given access to the files. Once the investigation is complete, the files should be stored so that the confidentiality of the information is maintained. Ensure that their files of closed investigations are stored safely and for as long as your company's document retention guidelines require.

Be observant about the details regarding the substance as well as the context and circumstances in which documents are prepared and maintained. Additionally, be alert to alterations, white-out areas, erased margin notes, earlier drafts and documents that should be present but are missing.

> **Process Pointer:** Interviews and document-gathering are only means to an end. The purpose is to give you the information needed to confront the implicated person and obtain admissions of wrongdoing.
>
> Don't slow the process down by trying to get every possible document that might be relevant. Just consider the scope of the investigation and the material facts you need to prove. Then ask yourself what documents cover those areas.

## M) Evidence Standards

Evidence consists of information, documents and objects that are used to prove or disprove facts. The investigator gathers evidence in order to determine the facts in the case. Although the investigative report will not directly address the evidence behind every fact stated in the report, the quality of that evidence eventually determines the degree to which the facts will be accepted by others. Rules of evidence exist to ensure evidence is reliable, and you should be familiar with and apply the more important rules and the concepts behind them.

Evidence includes information obtained from people, documents, and physical objects. Information from witnesses may be testimonial (oral descriptions of statements, acts, and events) or demonstrative. It may constitute first-hand knowledge of witnesses, or recitation of what they have learned from others (hearsay). Documents may be obtained merely to prove their existence (there was a contract), or to establish the substance of their contents (the contract was signed by a specific person, or it included a specific provision). Similarly, physical objects may be used to demonstrate their existence or identity (the serial number on the notebook computer found in a private residence establishes it is the company-owned property), or to demonstrate a particular characteristic or quality of the object that is in dispute.

## *Qualities of Evidence Used in Investigations*

Consider the following qualities of evidence in determining its value to the investigation:

**Relevance.** In obtaining and evaluating evidence, consider its relevance by asking whether it tends to make a fact that is of consequence to the investigation more probable than it would be without that evidence. If not, then the evidence is not relevant, and its incorporation into the investigative report is not appropriate. (The question of relevancy often arises in the consideration of circumstantial evidence.)

**Materiality.** Evidence is relevant if it tends to make an important fact more probable. A fact is material if it tends to prove or disprove an allegation. For example, the fact that vendor A's proposal was given to competing vendor B by Steve, a member of the Procurement Department, is material to proving an allegation that Steve violated company policy by leaking confidential information. The fact that Joan, another member of the department, also had a copy of the proposal is not likely to be material to the allegation against Steve (unless it can be used to suggest Joan, not Steve, was the source of the leak).

Evidence in the form of a statement by Larry that he saw Steve take the proposal out of the file cabinet and hand it to Nancy, an employee of vendor B, is relevant to establishing the fact that Steve really did give the proposal to vendor B. Larry's observation that Nancy was wearing a blue dress that day is not evidence that tends to make more likely the fact that Steve gave her the proposal (unless it is used to establish the person really was Nancy) and, therefore, that evidence is not relevant.

**Competence.** In obtaining and evaluating information, consider whether the circumstances by which it was obtained support a belief in its truthfulness. For example, statements by a witness with a history of lying, or impaired perception, or with a strong bias or prejudice, are likely to be of limited value in establishing facts. Similarly, a confession or statement containing information contrary to one's interest or benefit obtained under duress or a perception of coercion will not be as reliable as one obtained fairly and freely.

**Authenticity.** In obtaining and evaluating information, consider its authenticity - is it what it purports to be? Is the signature on the document really that of the person whose name it conveys? Could someone else have used the implicated person's computer name and password? Issues of authenticity are generally resolved by the quality (or lack) of chain of custody proof. The authenticity of testimony is also bolstered by being given under oath, such as with an affidavit.

## *Relevant Categories of Evidence*

You will deal with several categories of evidence and should understand the distinctions between them.

**Direct evidence.** Evidence, in whatever form, may tend to prove or disprove a fact either directly or indirectly (circumstantially). A fact is proved by direct evidence when the witness has actual, or direct, knowledge of the fact to be proved, and does not need to rely on facts the witness did not actually observe, but only inferred from other facts known to the witness. A witness who says, "I know that Mike stole the company checks because I was there with them, I saw Mike open the filing cabinet, take the checks and put them in his pocket" has presented direct evidence to prove the fact that Mike took the checks.

**Circumstantial evidence** - When direct evidence cannot be obtained to establish a fact, the existence of that fact may sometimes be established because reasonable persons are willing to draw inferences from other facts. Circumstantial evidence is direct evidence of one or more facts from which other facts may be inferred, or established indirectly, because there is a logical relationship between them. A witness who says, "I know Mike stole the checks because he was the only one in the room at about the time they were stolen," has presented circumstantial evidence to prove the fact that Mike stole the checks. The evidence is circumstantial because the witness did not actually observe Mike steal the checks, but inferred that fact from other facts the witness did observe directly. In the absence of other contrary facts, it is logical to infer that the only person in the room who had access to the checks likely stole them.

**Understanding the distinction.** It is important to appreciate the difference between direct and circumstantial evidence because circumstantial evidence has the possibility for an alternate explanation of what really happened. In the previous example, there may have been a second person in the office whom the witness did not see. Witnesses may think they know something directly, and present it in that manner, when in fact they are really drawing inferences from indirect, or circumstantial, evidence. When a witness says "I know fact A occurred" it is important to establish the actual basis for that assertion. Careful examination may show that the witness does not really know fact "A" occurred, but only that facts "B" and "C" did. Test a witness's statements by probing follow-up questions, such as, "why do you think that?" and, "how do you know that?" Don't reject evidence because it proves to be circumstantial, but remember that such evidence should be more critically evaluated and, when possible, corroborated with additional evidence.

**Fact versus opinion.** Opinions are generally conclusions premised on facts and the interpretation of those facts. For example, to say that Mike was shouting at Jim, was calling him names, and was red in the face, constitutes a recitation of facts. To merely state that Mike was angry at Jim constitutes an opinion that is based on the facts observed. The opinion may be accurate, but you cannot be certain without knowing the facts underlying it. Indeed, in some cases, observation of physical details may not always be sufficient to form a valid opinion. Jim may have been helping Mike practice a role in a play that required Mike to show anger.

**Limitation on use of opinion evidence.** Opinion testimony by laymen (people who are not "experts") is generally not admissible in court and, for similar reasons, has limited value in your investigation. When obtaining and evaluating evidence, recognize the distinction. Ask for the facts that underlie a witness's opinion. However, ordinary people form opinions about certain events as a result of their everyday experiences, and should be permitted to give their "opinions" as to those events. The most common example is permitting a lay witness to testify as to the speed of a moving vehicle. Remember that people become "experts" by experience as well as education and training.

### *Relevant Rules of Evidence*

The administrative and judicial proceedings which may result from a workplace investigation are generally governed by the Federal Rules of Evidence, either directly (because their application is mandatory in a federal district court) or indirectly because administrative boards (like the Equal

Employment Opportunity Commission) often look to them for general guidance. Many state courts use state-law evidence rules, which are often based entirely on the federal rules.

You should be familiar with some of these rules. The rules should be considered as substantive guidance about how to evaluate the evidence you develop in an investigation. All evidence is not the same.

## *Hearsay Evidence*

The Federal Rules of Evidence define hearsay as "a statement, other than one made by the declarant while testifying at the trial or hearing, offered in evidence to prove the truth of the matter asserted." The rules go on to explain that a statement constitutes hearsay only if three conditions are present:

- the evidence is an assertive statement or act;
- the statement or act was made or committed out of court; and
- the evidence is being used to prove the truth of the assertion.

Unless all three conditions are satisfied, the statement is not hearsay (and is therefore presumably competent).

Hearsay evidence is seldom admitted in a court proceeding unless it falls within one of the hearsay exceptions. This is because the declarant is not available for the type of examination, by the opposing party or the court, which would establish whether the statement may be relied upon. Hearsay evidence is generally admissible in proceedings like workplace investigations, but they should generally be given less weight than non-hearsay evidence.

Note that what a person says to you based on personal, direct knowledge may not be "hearsay" to you because you can probe the witness for problems with perception, memory, bias, etc. You also may base findings and conclusions on evidence that is hearsay, but be cautious in the use of this evidence, recognizing that you did not have an opportunity to test its reliability by interviewing the original source.

## *Statements against Interest*

When people make admissions, or other statements they know are likely to be detrimental to their interests, they are less likely to be lying than when they protest their innocence. Similarly, when innocent people are accused of wrongdoing, they generally deny it. Although there is some disagreement as to whether an out-of-court admission is hearsay, the Federal Rules say it is not. Thus, Carrie may testify in court that Mike told her he was the one who shot Jim, and this evidence may be used to prove the fact that Mike made the statement, to show Mike's state of mind at the time, and to prove the truth of the assertion itself. Similarly, Mike's silence when Carrie accuses him of shooting Jim may also be introduced through Carrie to prove that Mike shot Jim, as could Mike's response that Carrie was right. However, where circumstances indicate a person does not have a reasonable opportunity to deny the accusation, or has the right to remain silent (for example, when under arrest), silence should not be construed as an admission.

To establish the implicated person's acceptance of another person's accusation by silence, you should attempt to obtain facts that would show the following:

- The statement was made in the implicated person's presence and was in the form of an accusation against the implicated person;
- The implicated person heard and understood the accusation;
- The circumstances were such that an innocent person would deny the accusation; and
- The implicated person remained silent, or gave an evasive or equivocal response.

### *Business Records*

When a document is offered to prove the truth of the statements in it, it is hearsay. But bringing in all the witnesses necessary to prove the statements in a document can be unduly burdensome. Most business organizations have an interest in maintaining accurate records of the normal business they conduct regularly. When certain indicators of reliability are present in connection with the creation of a business record, the "business record exception" to the hearsay rule is used. Courts then recognize that the business record may be more accurate than the memories of the people who originally created it.

To establish whether a record was created in the ordinary course of business, you should attempt to determine:

1. Whether the document was prepared by a person with a business relationship with the company (usually an employee, but other people who have business with the company may also qualify);
2. Whether that person had personal knowledge of the facts or events recorded in the document;

3. Whether the document was prepared at a time reasonably close to the occurrence of the events;
4. Whether it is a routine practice of the company to prepare documents of this nature;
5. Whether the information recorded in the document is the type of information the company would ordinarily record in the regular course of its business; and
6. Whether the information is essentially factual in nature.

Note that the person who provides the document need not have personal knowledge of the information recorded in the document, and, in fact, usually does not have such information.

Having established the reliability of a business record by asking the questions presented in the preceding section, you still need to determine the authenticity of the particular document being provided. To do this, it is usually sufficient to establish proper custody of the document between the time it was created and the time it is presented to the investigator. You would want to know:

1. Whether the person providing the document has personal knowledge of the company's filing system;
2. The name (or description) of the file from which the person removed the document;
3. Whether the witness recognizes the document as one that should be contained in the file where it was located; and
4. In some cases, you may want to know who has access to the files, whether there is any reasonable possibility of tampering with the files, and the process through which a document goes from initial receipt to storage in the file.

## *Chain of Custody*

Chain of custody issues relate to proving the authenticity of objects. If you must account for objects of this nature, be prepared to establish the following points:

1. The object has a unique characteristic;
2. The witness observed the characteristic on a previous occasion;
3. The witness looks at the object and identifies it as the one seen earlier; and

4. The witness points out the unique characteristic that leads him to conclude the object is the one seen earlier.

To establish that an object was not substituted or altered, each step in the movement of the object must be traced in such manner as to establish that:
1. The witness originally received the object at a certain time and place;
2. The witness safeguarded the object while in his or her possession in order to prevent substitution or tampering;
3. The witness eventually disposed of the object in some manner (usually by turning it over to the next person in the chain);
4. As best the witness can tell, the object he or she is now looking at is the object the witness previously handled; and
5. As best the witness can tell, the object is in the same condition as when the witness originally received it.

The Federal Rules of Evidence do not apply to workplace investigations, because the investigation is not a lawsuit. But the rules remain useful to investigators because the rules rank evidence quality and explain distinctions that you should remember. All proof is not the same. All witnesses are not equal. By understanding the differences in evidence, you can ensure that your investigation proof is as strong as possible to support your findings.

## N) Reaching a Conclusion

When you have finished gathering evidence, management should be notified, and you should generally be available to answer any questions. You should express appreciation for the support received, and indicate whether there were any significant problems that hindered the conduct of the investigation. You should also advise management whether the climate suggested a concern over retaliation for cooperating with you. You should not comment on the substance of the findings, noting that the investigation is not considered complete until the investigative report is completed. Management may be advised of the general timeframe in which to expect the report to be finalized, and who to contact for a status update.

### *Deciding what Happened*

Most investigations collect more information than is necessary to reach a conclusion. Some information is redundant; other information is not pertinent to a decision. Sometimes the information is conflicting. Deciding what information to treat as evidence and how to deal with it in the investigation report is important because in cases where remedial or disciplinary action is a possibility, the decision to accept the conclusions in the investigation report is likely to be made only after an examination of all the evidentiary material in the file. If the report does not appear to fairly address pertinent evidence, its conclusions may be rejected. Some common issues in deciding what happen include:

- Evidence considered, but not relied upon, should be discussed in the investigation report if it is likely that others would want to consider it, or question the completeness of the report were it not mentioned. This is critical when there is conflicting evidence.
- The failure to discuss and explain why one version of events is relied upon in lieu of competing evidence will cause readers who are aware of the conflicts to question the objectivity of the writer.
- Evidence that is redundant or repetitive can be summarized when it comes from various sources that present no unique information. For example, stating that five people saw the implicated person in the office on a particular day is adequate in most cases.
- Testimony may prove difficult to analyze in some cases. Often, only a few witnesses have the entire story. You must piece together fragments of the story to present the entire picture. Summarizing the testimony of witnesses providing these fragments is one acceptable technique to make the sequence of events clear. In complex cases, or cases with many witnesses, it is helpful to use some system for identifying what each witness said about each allegation, such as an evidence matrix or an outline.

The evidentiary analysis must bring together all documentary, physical, and testimonial facts relating to the allegations to reach a conclusion. The facts relied upon to reach each conclusion should be apparent to the reader. When the applicable standards are themselves vague, or the testimony conflicts, the reasoning that leads to a conclusion is not always apparent. In that case, the analysis in the investigation report must explain to the reader how you reached the conclusion.

Don't forget to consider the "root cause" of why something happened. The root cause may be that the implicated person didn't know the rule, could not comply with it, and/or would not comply with it.

## Only Three Outcomes

Considering the stakes involved, you have to make a finding. It is neither professional nor helpful to your company if you remain perplexed and simply shrug your shoulders as to the investigation outcome. You must make a decision, and there are only three possibilities:

- **Substantiated.** A substantiated finding results when a preponderance of the evidence supports the allegation of misconduct. The facts, from documentation and testimony, indicate that a violation occurred.
- **Unsubstantiated.** An unsubstantiated finding results when (i) a preponderance of the evidence supports the conclusion that the alleged misconduct did not occur, or (ii) the available evidence is insufficient to meet the burden of proof, even if you believe that the misconduct occurred.
- **Inconclusive.** An inconclusive finding results in the rare situation where you simply cannot complete the investigation, for example because of the unavailability of witnesses and/or essential documents.

## Reporting the Findings

Sometimes, business managers would rather not see anything in writing. This view should be unacceptable to executive management and certainly to you. There are a variety of methods available to the company to ensure a limited distribution of an investigative report. The first time an investigative report is suppressed for the purpose of avoiding a proper review by management marks the beginning of the end of the integrity of your process. The outcome of the investigation must provide answers to the "magic questions" of the investigation: who, what, where, when, why and how. The detail provided should be sufficient to explain your business processes to someone who is unfamiliar with the business. If you accurately tell the story in the fewest words, you stand a better chance of having the report reviewed.

As companies increasingly view compliance professionals as business counselors, reporting the findings is the best opportunity to demonstrate the value of the workplace investigations process to your company. You need good communications abilities, problem-solving skills, knowledge of the business and client-partnership skills.

# O) The Final Report

The purpose of the workplace investigation's final investigative report (known colloquially as the "Final Report") is to demonstrate why the allegations investigated were (or were not) sustained, in order to provide the responsible managers a basis to determine whether any corrective, remedial, or disciplinary action should be taken. A well-written Final Report "tells a story" to the reader as it discusses the nature of the allegations, explains the applicable standards, and assembles the pertinent facts in order to persuade the reader that the investigator's conclusions are correct. Objectivity and basic fairness also require that the Final Report provide a balanced accounting of evidence that might tend to support a contrary conclusion, and explain why such evidence was not accorded greater weight. The ability to balance these competing considerations is the hallmark of a professional—and legally defensible—Final Report.

> **Process Pointer:** Writing a Final Report is not easy. But it represents a critical element of a good investigation. It gives your investigation credibility. If the report is poor, you risk ruining an otherwise good investigation.
>
> Let someone else decide the consequences from the meaning of the facts. Remember that you are just a presenter of the proof you gathered. If you are tempted to offer a conclusion or opinion on consequences, it is probably because your Final Report is not clear enough, and you are trying to help the reader along. If you gathered good evidence, the proof will speak for itself without your help.

## *The Final Report's Structure*

A written report creates a lasting record of the findings and allows management to consider its contents over time. A written report is a persuasive way to communicate that misconduct did (or did not) occur or that corrective action has already been taken. The report also provides support for the company's resolution of the matter, and it shows that the company's investigative process was objective and neutral. Finally, the report constitutes the company's "stake in the ground;" the company has committed to these facts when making its decision regarding how to proceed. A template of a Final Report may be found in Appendix M.

The Final Report is limited to analyzing the facts within the scope of the investigation. The scope should also be clearly specified in the report. The report's recommendations and findings should be limited by that scope as well. This will provide a clear understanding to anyone to whom the report is disclosed regarding the investigation's boundaries. Later on, if additional facts develop, you may need to explain why the findings in the Final Report were comparatively narrow and did not cover the areas under scrutiny. Without a scope specified in the Final Report, your investigation may look incomplete (or that your investigation sidestepped some areas of inquiry).

Once your fact-finding is done and you have made your recommendations, you are ready to draft the Final Report. A typical Final Report has the following elements:

- The nature of the report and how it was brought to your attention;
- A summary of the facts gathered throughout the investigation, including a chronology of events. This is a neutral narrative of the key events uncovered by the investigation;
- The people interviewed and the documents reviewed;
- A brief discussion of any credibility assessments reached;
- What created the opportunity, and how much opportunity did the subject have;
- Whether the report was substantiated or unsubstantiated or the results were inconclusive. If substantiated, what conclusions are supported by what was found;
- The specific conclusion(s) reached on each key issue;
- The identification of any issues that could not be resolved in the investigation;
- A brief discussion of how the company guidelines or policies apply to the situation;
- Whether applicable controls were adequate or circumvented;
- Whether any relevant compliance controls were followed to prevent other problems or reduce the impact;
- How long the problem has gone on, and what, if any, is the financial impact to the company or third parties;
- How the company is responding to the report, if it is substantiated; and
- A list of the key documents used in the investigation.

> **Process Pointer:** You must compile the facts into a theory about what happened and tell a story. Facts alone prove little. The mathematician Henri Poincare once said: "Science is built up with facts, as a house is with stones. But a collection of facts is no more a science than a heap of stones is a house."

## *Best Practices*

Regardless of the format you choose, there are some basic considerations to ensure the content of the report is helpful. Keep it simple and factual. Facts make up the backbone of all reports.

A proper Final Report offers no recommendations on how an offending employee should be disciplined, whether the company should compensate someone, or similar possible post-investigation actions. Those steps are outside the scope of the investigation. Also, if you can decide on the resulting disciplinary action to be taken, a conflict of interest may be created that interferes with your ability to find the objective truth of what happened. However, the Final Report may include recommendations for additional investigation and corrective changes to the business' operations.

Use the first person singular when referring to yourself. Using the third person is awkward and should be avoided. Be direct in your explanations.

Strive for clarity and accuracy. Words create expectations that add to or detract from any writing. Appreciate the implications of your words and how they could be unintentionally misconstrued. Remember that words carry meanings, including provocative ones.

The report should never contain your opinions. It should not state, for example, that "Steve Smith appeared uninterested." Rather, it should state that "Steve Smith continually looked around the room and requested that questions be repeated to him two or three times before he would answer."

The report must explicitly and precisely describe any documents that are part of the findings. Do not use phrases like "the records include the following…" because that implies that there are other records besides the ones mentioned.

The report must reach conclusions, even when it might seem difficult to do so. Assess the credibility of the witnesses. Examine the objective facts and consider motivations. State each of these factors clearly and explicitly.

However, do not use emphasis—such as, "the manager was thoroughly incompetent" -- when expressing findings or conclusions.

Factual assumptions should be described specifically and in detail. There should be no guessing regarding the factual assumptions upon which a finding is based. Avoid terms like "supposedly" and "presumably."

The Final Report should use direct quotes whenever possible. Quoting a witness directly strengthens the factual assertions.

Be careful when using pronouns. Be clear so that the reader can be sure to whom or what they refer.

When possible, the report should refer to relevant company policies, practices and written procedures. This grounds the factual context within the operations of the business.

Avoid expressing opinions, because opinions can easily be challenged. Once doubt is brought to opinions expressed in the report, the credibility of the report and investigation may also be challenged. It is better to focus on what the facts show, rather than what the investigator personally concludes from the inquiries.

Avoid inflammatory or judgmental words. The report is intended to gather facts only, not pass judgments on others.

Stick to company business and not, for example, observations of personal conduct outside of the office. The scope of the report should be focused on the specific issues under investigation.

Your tone should be respectful, courteous and constructive, even if you think that a witness was lying to you or the substantiated misconduct was egregious.

The Final Report should be written as if it will be published. The report might be included in documents that are more widely circulated.

Do not make legal conclusions about any perceived law violations, breaches of contract, or potential liability. These conclusions are outside the scope of the investigation. You may also not have the competence to make those conclusions (or they are beyond your job duties).

Do not include any of your observations or similar conclusions that could be construed as admissions of company liability. If a witness makes a statement that could be construed as such, and you believe that the statement should be included, be sure to attribute the statement clearly: "Steve Smith stated in his interview that he believed that this violated the law."

The Final Report should specify any contradictions that surfaced during the interview. Contradictions can exist between documents and interviews, among different witnesses or when the witness contradicts himself. Indicate whether, through your efforts, you were able to resolve any conflicts in testimony or documents. Otherwise, unresolved contradictions may reflect negatively on your investigation.

If an acknowledgement, admission or confession is made, be specific as to exactly what was admitted. If the individual acknowledged doing two things, you should write out exactly what happened so that a reader cannot possibly incorrectly believe that he admitted to doing ten or only one.

The Final Report should not report your conclusions about the merits of the allegations or offer an opinion on what, if any, action should be taken regarding the subject of the investigation or a witness.

Be brief, but tell a complete story. Write for an educated audience, but not someone who is knowledgeable about that part of the business. Define all technical terms, jargon and acronyms. (The Final Report may, after all, end up being distributed outside your company.)

The ultimate test of a good Final Report is simply this: if the reader of the report still has a question after reading it, the report is probably deficient in some way.

---

**Process Pointer:** Do not make recommendations regarding disciplinary action. It probably creates a conflict of interest, because it will create the appearance that you tailored your findings to support your recommendation. Offer the findings and let others decide what to do with them.

Use care when communicating the results of an investigation. Be certain that the person who asks for it has a justifiable business purpose for knowing the information. The company can be liable for over-disseminating the investigation results.

Never put your opinions in the final report. If doubt is later cast on the validity of your opinion, then that doubt will undermine the credibility of your report and the underlying investigation. Focus instead on what the facts show, rather than your own personal insights, however valid and accurate they might be.

## Style and Tone

Whether the allegations are sustained or refuted, most Final Reports convey bad news to someone. Proper style and tone makes the news easier to accept; an inappropriate style or tone impedes acceptance and appropriate resolution. Style varies from one person to another, but a simple, direct approach, without colorful language, is the most effective way to convey facts. The tone should be neutral, not judgmental, convincing in its modesty of language, not provocative in its descriptions. Style, tone and clarity must complement one another; each handled well tends to achieve the others.

## Discussing the Allegations

This section is the heart of the Final Report. Each allegation is usually discussed separately. The order of presentation of the allegations should facilitate an overall understanding of the case. Sometimes the allegations are discussed in chronological order of the facts pertinent to each allegation. In other cases, allegations that are conceptually linked, or share common facts, should be placed close together. When the order of presentation is not critical to an overall understanding of the case, then it is common to list the most important in terms of seriousness or sensitivity first. Among those, it is typical to discuss first those allegations that were sustained, then those that were not sustained. Allegations that were neither sustained nor refuted should appear last. Allegations should be worded in the same manner as they were during issue spotting and specified in the investigative plan. The reporter's language may be used if it facilitates an understanding of the issues, but be sure to attribute the language to the reporter (using direct quotes when possible).

## Presenting the Findings

The findings present and analyze the evidence you developed and decided to address in the report with respect to each allegation. Organization and content of the findings are critical to a good report.

Good report organization facilitates understanding by an unfamiliar reader. A chronological statement of facts is most likely to achieve this objective. One approach is to set forth the standard, followed by a chronology, or vice versa. When a chronology is not important, setting forth information that tends to support the allegation, then information that tends to refute the allegation, promotes understanding. Where there is substantial disagreement over the facts, it may be helpful to first explain the reporter's story, followed by the implicated person's version. Facts provided by neutral parties should follow, ending with a discussion that reconciles or selects between conflicting facts.

To promote objectivity, the implicated person's response to the allegations should be specified, to include the implicated person's interpretation of the rule or standard alleged to have been violated and the implicated person's motivation when those issues are pertinent.

Completeness requires that all significant evidence, pro or con, be discussed. The pertinent standard must also be set out and, where necessary, explained. Persuasiveness requires that the logical chain between the statement of facts and the conclusions are clearly specified in the Final Report.

## *The Discussion*

The discussion in the Final Report explains the weight you assign to the facts set forth in the findings and how they fit together to substantiate or refute the allegations. Consequently, when the issues surrounding an allegation are simple and facts are not in dispute, this section may not be necessary. It should never include new facts, and it should not restate facts already detailed in the findings. Rather, you should sift through the facts in conflict and reconcile them, if possible. If conflicting facts cannot be reconciled, you must explain why one version of the facts is found to be more credible than another. In some cases, this may simply consist of comparing the number of witnesses who say an event happened to the number who say it did not and going with the majority vote. In most cases, however, questions of perception, bias, self-interest, competence, and veracity must be addressed, because it is the quality of the evidence, not the quantity, that determines how disputed issues should be resolved.

## *The Conclusions*

Each allegation must have one or more conclusions, which must be consistent with, and flow logically from, the findings and discussion. Where facts are in dispute, the discussion should make obvious the reasons for the conclusions. Therefore, no further discussion in the conclusions section should be necessary if the allegation is substantiated or not substantiated. When an allegation is partially substantiated, the conclusion must clearly distinguish those portions that were substantiated from those that were not.

When an allegation is substantiated, but extenuating or mitigating circumstances are present, they should be discussed, i.e. "... however, the facts indicate implicated person was motivated by concern for subordinates and not self-interest." The conclusions may also reflect that an allegation, as framed in the Final Report, was not substantiated, but that a related allegation would be. An example is the case where the allegation of an actual conflict of interest is not substantiated, but the appearance of a conflict does exist.

## *Recommendations to Management*

The recommendations section should contain constructive suggestions for action by the responsible managers. Every Final Report should contain a recommendation as to the status of the investigation, i.e., that it be closed as completed based on the report, or that further action along specific lines such as that raised in the other matters section be taken.

Where the Final Report has identified systemic problems or program weaknesses, a recommendation to consider corrective action to "fix the system" is appropriate. A general recommendation for remedial action may also be included, but specific recommendations for adverse administrative or disciplinary action should not appear in the Final Report. In such cases, the recommendation should merely indicate that "appropriate action" should be taken with regard to the implicated person or suspect.

## *Common Errors in Final Reports*

Problems in Final Reports often occur because investigators know the case so well that they fail to include information in the Final Report that readers who are not familiar with the case need to know. Other problems occur because of sloppy writing habits or the failure to organize and place information in the appropriate sections of the report. Some common investigator errors include the following:

**Mixing up facts, opinions, and conclusions.** There are separate sections of the Final Report for recording facts, opinions, and conclusions. All too often, writers give their opinions in the middle of a recitation of facts. This is confusing and may cause readers to question whether the investigator understands the difference. Opinions may creep in through the use of adjectives and adverbs in a sentence setting forth facts. This may occur because the investigator fails to reserve the discussion of the implications that may be drawn from the facts for a later section of the report. Another common problem is the inclusion of facts, for the first time in the report, in the sections of the report reserved for conclusions and recommendations. This often happens when the investigator realizes that a fact necessary to support the conclusion does not appear in the findings section.

**Unsupported conclusions.** Sometimes it is not apparent how the investigator arrived at the conclusions based on the evidence presented in the Final Report. This usually occurs for one of three reasons. First, because investigators are so familiar with the case, they may think they included a fact when they did not, or they may assume something will be apparent to the reader that is not obvious to one unfamiliar with the investigation. In most cases, the evidence was gathered, it simply was not reported.

A second reason is the inclusion of conflicting statements of fact that were not resolved in the discussion of the findings. When the reader looks at some of the reported facts, the conclusions appear logical, but when others are added, a contrary result would also appear reasonable. This requires the reader to attempt to resolve the conflicts, often without any information in the report that would provide a logical basis for doing so.

A third reason is the failure to cite and, where necessary, discuss the standard that should be applied to the facts in order to reach a conclusion. The most effective way to avoid these problems is to adhere to the outline of proof in the investigative plan when writing, then to ask someone in the office who is unfamiliar with the case to read a draft of the Final Report.

**Conclusions that just cannot be supported.** Misinterpreting testimony, misreading documents, and not wording allegations properly may result in erroneous conclusions for which there is simply no support in the investigative record. This discredits recommendations and damages the integrity of the investigation process. This problem may not be obvious from a reading of the Final Report itself; it is most likely to be discovered when management is reviewing the Final Report to determine whether or not it will support disciplinary action.

To avoid this situation, you first must be able to document the source of every fact in the report. The most effective way to do so is to create an endnote for each statement of fact when writing the draft of the Final Report. The end-noted draft should be maintained in the file; the endnotes should not appear in the Final Report. Using endnotes permits another person in the office to quickly review the document, interview notes, or other sources of evidence relied on to support the facts in order to determine if there is sufficient support in the record.

**Recommendations not consistent with conclusions.** Occasionally, conclusions are presented that merit a recommendation, but none appears in the Final Report. In other cases, the conclusion does not support the recommendation. These errors are likely to be picked up when drafts are reviewed by compliance colleagues not familiar with the case.

## *Management Response to the Final Report*

The final step in the investigation process is for the company to implement corrective action. Ensure that management has met with the person who was the subject of the investigation as well as the employee who raised the issue.

Remedial action must be proper and prompt. Internal remedial steps could include revising corporate procedures or management structures, revising compliance procedures or oversight, as well as employee disciplinary action. It might also include specifying best practices and increasing employee training. External remedial steps could include disclosures in public filings and compensating injured third parties.

The Final Report will also facilitate everyone's attention and agreement regarding the substantiated problem. The discovered problem may trigger an audit to prevent future and more serious problems.

The Final Report may have collateral value to the company. If the report is used in a private litigation, the findings can defend the company from certain claims. Because the report will contain specific findings of fact and the bases for the findings, the report can be used as a guide to resolve the dispute informally. These uses, however, must be balanced against the risks of waiving applicable legal privileges, identifying wrongdoers and the sources of information, and the possibility that the report may be circulated beyond the company's control.

If the misconduct—or the perception of misconduct that was actually proper behavior—was seen to have impacted a wider group of people, such as the implicated employee's department, a manager may want to debrief the work group. The debriefing could take the form of bringing all employees together at the same time in a meeting format. This lets everyone have the same information about the allegations, the scope and results of the investigation, and what, if any, changes may be made in the workplace. Debriefing meetings can be an effective method for neutralizing rumors and miscommunications among employees. They also provide the opportunity to reinforce company policies and management directives.

After the meeting, and in those circumstances where appropriate, managers should send the affected staff a memo reminding them about your company's policy against retaliation. A sample memo may be found in Appendix N.

## P) Executive Summaries

Investigations defy easy quantification. Don't place too much stock in the persuasive effect of your statistics. As to a specific case, decision-makers are not likely to focus on a specific investigation of yours unless it is a significant one. But it is important to cultivate these people as your allies. After all, your investigations protect their business interests.

A simple way to show them your value is to send a monthly executive summary to key business leaders in your company. The summary should include a status report on each investigation that remains pending as of the date of your summary. Mention what you have uncovered so far, and state your overall objective for the investigation. Objectives include identifying contributory fault by third-parties, as well as identifying process deficiencies. Remind them indirectly that substantiating the misconduct is just one part of what you are doing.

Give a full summary of any closed investigations. This would include substantiated cases, unsubstantiated cases, and inconclusive ones. State your findings and whether other departments assisted the investigation. If there were breakdowns in the process, say so. State any "lessons learned" in order to underscore the investigation's relevance to the business. If you expect any future steps to be taken, such as a referral to law enforcement, be sure to mention it.

## Q) Business Ethics Bulletins

Another way to increase your visibility within the company is to disseminate information about specific investigations that yielded important operational information. By showcasing compliance violation cases and subsequent penalties, you are highlighting the company's commitment to ethical standards and necessary corrective action. The perception that the company is committed to upholding the standards enhances employee belief in ethics messages.

Ethics bulletins serve as awareness and education tools by providing real-world examples of corporate violations. These examples resonate more fully with employees than hypothetical, abstract training examples. For example, some investigations identify specific procedural flaws—unsecured company property, insufficient safeguards on sensitive information, unsupervised employees—that are likely to be recurring elsewhere. Using the investigation's factual findings (or a sterilized version of them) can give the readers a practical example of what happened and what they need to do to prevent it from happening to them. It will make the information more meaningful than just an abstract admonition to be careful. A sample bulletin may be found in Appendix O.

Your business ethics bulletins should follow each of these principles; the bulletin should:
- Be clear, concise and easy to read;
- Never identify involved employees by name;
- State how the activity was uncovered;
- Relate specific facts regarding the activity or offense to help prevent future occurrences of a similar nature;
- Give relevant and specific facts regarding the investigation;
- Emphasize the importance of adhering to the company's code of conduct, regardless of the amount at issue (if the offense appears to be of a small dollar amount);
- Mention any instances of reluctant or refused cooperation with investigators in order to stress the importance of full cooperation;
- State the specific policy violated and the result;
- Offer a key takeaways section that is as concrete and specific as possible.

An added benefit of the bulletin is that it reminds your colleagues in the other departments that you exist for more than just answering calls to the whistleblower hotline. Increased visibility may also encourage them to alert you directly in the future.

> **Process Pointer:** The process requires you to prepare the Final Report, but other documents such as summaries and bulletins help convey the information so that it can be used by your business colleagues to improve operations. Think about how your information can be most effectively presented. After all, if the information is not conveyed in an effective way, your process will also be seen as ineffective.

## R) Reporting to the Reporter

When the investigation is complete, you need to inform the reporter accordingly. In some cases, the reporter will be an employee of your company, but the reporter may also be an outsider. Either way, you need to be able to explain that the investigation was completed in a commercially reasonable way, and that the process is done. Unless you respond, the perception will be that the initial report was not investigated, and that it fell down some black hole in the corporate bureaucracy. A response closes the process, reinforces its fairness, and it may anticipate (or preempt) the contact by a dissatisfied reporter to your executive management, a regulator or the media.

However, you must remember not to breach your confidentiality obligations, and you should not disclose anything that could be construed as your (inadvertent) admission of company liability. The easiest approach is usually (i) to thank the reporter for reporting the matter to you; (ii) to tell them that the investigation is now complete; and (iii) to convey that any corrective action, if necessary, will be promptly taken. Don't disclose whether the allegation was substantiated or what disciplinary action may be taken against employees. The reporter only has a reasonable expectation to be informed that their concerns were handled appropriately. A sample response to the reporter may be found in Appendix P.

# PART III
## Other Investigation Issues

### A) Special Concerns of Investigation

An overriding principle in conducting workplace investigations is "do no harm." Problems have been made worse by poor investigations that make the investigation process look incompetent at best and as a cover-up at worst.

All workplace investigations have risks. Be mindful of possible tort claims arising from how the investigation is conducted, regardless of its outcome.

*Unethical Investigator Behavior*
Unethical investigator behavior undermines any value that the process brings to the company. It damages the quality of investigations as well as the respect the compliance professionals enjoy within the company. Any of the following behaviors are unacceptable:
- Selectively opening, closing, rushing or stalling an investigation based on a relationship with or pressure from a reporter, implicated person, witness or executive;
- Improperly handling evidence to influence the outcome of an investigation;
- Improperly handling evidence or testimony through incompetence, carelessness or lack of training;
- Fabricating information;
- Using interrogation tactics instead of interviewing tactics (except where appropriate);
- Treating each witness as though he is culpable, with little or no regard for the damage inflicted on blameless people;

- Making inappropriate threats or promises to employees;
- Compromising sensitive information or disclosing it improperly.

Unethical behavior exposes the company to civil and criminal liability. Make ethics a pillar of your operations. Ethical behavior enhances the value of your investigations rather than hindering it.

## *Opening Pandora's Box*

When a company is a victim of employee misconduct, and when that misconduct becomes public, the company faces harm beyond its immediate losses. For example, an investigation may be so effective in discovering misconduct that it develops information that might never have otherwise been learned by government or private litigants. The investigation process may also encourage disgruntled employees to make accusations that otherwise would not be disclosed. The investigation likely disrupts company operations. Finally, the investigation may create adverse publicity or internal divisiveness by employees who are being asked to report on the conduct of their colleagues.

## *Common Investigator Errors*

There is no single way to conduct a proper investigation. Methods vary depending on investigators and investigations. Despite these differing methods, some common problems may arise:

**Promptness.** Companies should not wait too long to investigate. This may result from delays in contacting reporters, referring the matter to investigators or delays in management reporting the matter to you. Delays compromise witness recollections and other proof. Delays also undermine employee confidence because delays may imply that the company does not care.

**Impartiality.** Companies may use an investigator who is somehow vested in the outcome of the investigation. This could be an investigator who is connected to the incidents under investigation (such as a Human Resources manager who has dealt with the parties before). It could be an investigator who is in the management hierarchy for that business group and might feel pressure to sway findings towards what he thinks his bosses expect. You may not be neutral in the outcome of the investigation. If your neutrality is compromised, so is the investigation. Even an investigation conducted to "clear" a subject may be compromised by an investigation's bias to reach a particular finding.

**Confidentiality.** You must maintain confidentiality of the subject and the witnesses to the extent possible. This must be balanced against the need to conduct a thorough investigation and to afford the subject a full opportunity to respond. The investigator must be sure that the investigation is not compromised by witnesses talking to or trying to influence others.

**Training.** A common error is the use of untrained—or under-trained—investigators. Do not choose someone who has little understanding of the substantive issues and no training or experience in conducting investigations and making credibility determinations. Experience acquired on the job is not a substitute for training. It may just be accumulated bad habits.

**Thoroughness.** Inexperienced investigators often have trouble understanding who they should interview, and in what order. They also frequently do not know how far to go. Their investigations may be merely superficial—emphasizing process over substance—with few witnesses interviewed and no real attempt to determine the facts. Conversely, they may wish to talk to every witness who has been mentioned in the investigation because they fear overlooking something.

**Questioning.** This is a critical part of the investigation process. Some investigators may ask questions that are too narrow. There is nothing wrong with asking narrow questions, but narrow questions elicit a different response than open-ended questions. Poorly trained investigators may ask few questions. They may simply ask the reporter to tell his or her side of the story, and then they may do the same with the subject of the investigation. These investigators usually do not understand the law and the fact issues.

**Determining Credibility.** Untrained investigators frequently are unable to determine credibility, and sometimes do not even try to do so. Even where it is one word against another and differing witness accounts cannot resolve the matter, you must still resolve credibility issues.

**Making a Determination.** Sometimes it is the word of one witness against another, and their stories are diametrically opposed. Some investigators simply conclude, as a result, that no determination can be made. There may be times when you cannot decide what you think happened. But this should be the exception and not the rule. You are expected to make a determination in your investigation. Typically, a number of people are depending on your findings.

Do not avoid reaching a conclusion out of the fear of being wrong. Unless your implicated person has admitted each of the material facts, you have no choice. Reach a reasonable conclusion as to the matters under investigation. As we know, this does not mean that it has to be the same amount of certainty that would apply in a criminal prosecution.

**Offering Opinions.** Do not offer opinions regarding the guilt or innocence of anyone involved. Observations are permissible, but the focus should be on whether the facts elicited during the investigation make your conclusions self-evident.

These errors may, in some jurisdictions, lead to claims for negligent investigation. Even if the claim cannot be made, the results of the investigation are compromised because of these mistakes.

> **Process Pointer:** By understanding the legal landmines, a conscientious investigator can step carefully in his pursuit of relevant information.

## *Poor Planning*

The investigation must be well-planned and executed with a definite objective and strategy. The failure to plan each step of the investigation and consider the potential consequences of each step places the company at risk for serious problems including:

- Damage to the company's reputation;
- Damage to employee morale;
- Damage to the company's compliance efforts;
- Creation of evidence that can be used in future criminal or civil cases;
- Possible full-blown government investigation and sanctions;
- Provision of no protection in private litigation;
- Enabling the possibility of future misconduct;
- Waste of company resources.

## *Obstruction of Justice*

Responding to allegations of misconduct requires skill to avoid making a bad situation worse. Obstruction of justice arises when the government is involved, and the government's inquiries are somehow impeded or hindered.

If improper or careless methods are used in a workplace investigation, it might appear later on as if the company was trying to cover up violations or distort a witness's testimony.

## *Compounding a Felony*

The right to punish or to forgive a criminal is reserved to the state and federal governments. Individual and corporate victims do not have the right to do that. Agreeing to accept something of value in return for not prosecuting—or for not reporting the crime to prosecutors—is itself a crime. It can result in legal problems for both the investigator and the company.

> **Process Pointer:** In some states, the promise not to report the matter to the police in exchange for something of value—money or information—is also considered extortion. It is a crime. Never promise the implicated person that you will or will not contact the police. Make your decision independent of his assistance, fears or preferences.

## *Whistleblower Protection*

A variety of federal and state laws exist to protect whistleblowers. If an investigation shows that someone who is a whistleblower is also someone who completely fabricated a claim to harass another person, the company should still weigh the effects and application of any whistleblower statute that may apply. A possible situation may involve a person who has properly engaged in some improper conduct and fears that it is about to be discovered. The reporter may file a whistleblower claim with managers to cloak themselves in the whistleblower protections.

## *Retaliation*

Those who are the source of a report and those who cooperate in an investigation are legally protected from retaliation. (This is in addition to the protections given by your company policies.) Ensure that the company does not take any unwarranted action against the employee that might appear to be retaliation for filing a report or cooperating with an investigation. Regardless of the legal implications of retaliation, the practical effect is that employees will only provide information in an investigation if they believe that they will not be penalized for doing so. When you investigate, remain alert to any signs of retaliation.

Retaliation may take a variety of forms:
- A negative performance evaluation;
- A failure to receive a promotion;
- Receiving lower quality work assignments;
- Being excluded from meetings and decision making;
- A reduced level of salary increase, bonus or other pay treatment;
- Being openly criticized or ostracized by colleagues or a manager.

You should be sufficiently conscious to the risk of retaliation and how to deal with it:
- Anticipate in your investigation who may be the target of possible retaliation.
- Remind the relevant managers of individuals who may be the target of retaliatory behavior to be aware of the risk and of their obligation to prevent and/or stop retaliation of any kind.
- Remind each person interviewed that any person who, in good faith, seeks advice, raises a concern, reports misconduct or cooperates in an investigation is following the company's code of conduct and doing the right thing.
- Make sure each witness understands the company's non-retaliation policy, and that the company will enforce it vigorously.
- If an individual alleges that he has been the victim of retaliation, the Investigations Manager or your compliance officer should be contacted immediately.

## *Discrimination*

The workplace investigations process must be consistently applied. This can be a particular problem when the process is first implemented, and where discipline is imposed in situations where it had not been before. Differences in treatment of employees invite allegations of discrimination of one form or another. There is also the risk that the sanctions applied later on to particular types of violations could have a disparate impact on the workforce and add to the appearance of discrimination.

When investigating claims of discrimination in the workplace, investigators must avoid the risk of discriminating themselves. For example, a worker complaining of religious discrimination may, in turn, claim that the employer engaged in religious discrimination by willingly failing to conduct an adequate investigation. Conversely, over-investigating could lead to complaints of "profiling" certain employees as possible investigation targets.

> **Process Pointer:** The failure to conduct a reasonable investigation risks a lawsuit by the implicated person—or even an implicated person in another similar investigation—for a variety of legal claims.

### *Invasion of Privacy*

During investigative interviews, especially those involving sexual harassment, investigators may have to explore sensitive areas of personal conduct. Recognize and appreciate your employees' reasonable expectations of privacy. Questioning employees concerning activities that are not sufficiently related to their conduct at work may constitute an invasion of privacy. Violating the right of privacy exposes the company to liability. The key here is to be cautious.

This claim generally has three elements: (i) an intentional intrusion, (ii) upon the claimant's private affairs or concerns, and (iii) that a reasonable person would find offensive. A well-recognized defense to an invasion-of-privacy claim is consent. However, the truth of the information is not the same thing as consent. Companies should draft appropriate policies and procedures to minimize privacy expectations. Initiate investigations only on the basis of documented factual allegations that objectively justify the investigation, rather than gossip, innuendo or "urban legend." Narrow the scope of any investigation to what is reasonable and necessary to protect the company's business interests. Finally, the information should be kept confidential and shared only with those who need to know it. Remember that your company has a legitimate right to conduct investigations in the workplace, but that right must be balanced against the rights of employees.

### *Defamation*

Investigators must be sensitive to the risks of defamation claims. Investigators must be careful not to draw unwarranted conclusions or make unfounded accusations against investigation subjects. Defamatory communication is communication which, among other things, injures that person's reputation as to diminish respect, goodwill or confidence in which that person is held. Defamation may arise in the context of investigation-related communications. Communicating those conclusions and accusations to third parties constitutes "publication" of that information for defamation purposes. This can include warning statements, investigative reports, performance evaluations and statements in management meetings.

To minimize this risk, investigators should explicitly detail the factual basis for any conclusions about an employee's culpability. Cautionary language should be used where possible. Supporting facts should be verified. The conclusions drawn should be reasonably justified by the facts. Do not use caustic, hyperbolic or otherwise colorful language. The report should also be distributed on a limited basis to avoid a claim of excessive publication.

Truth is a defense to a defamation claim. A qualified privilege may also exist where the statement was believed by the employer in good faith when it was made, the statement served a legitimate purpose, the statement was limited in scope, and was "published" to an individual who also had a legitimate business interest in receiving the communication. Additionally, the company must not have reason to believe that the statements or questions are false and must not be acting with reckless disregard for the truth. But the company must also not exceed the scope of that privilege. Careful investigating, especially the reporting or discussion of investigation findings, reduces the risk to the company.

### *Libel*

Many of the same considerations regarding defamation also apply to a possible libel claim. Useful investigation reports are both meticulous and frank. Questionable activities must be described in detail. In some investigations, the factual descriptions will be the equivalent of accusing someone of a crime or at least dishonesty.

### *False Imprisonment*

An employee establishes a claim for false imprisonment when an employee establishes that he was confined unreasonably during the investigation. The risk of such a claim during an investigation is greatest when the subject is being interviewed. You have the authority to question employees regarding conduct connected at work, and your company should require cooperation as a condition of employment. However, you may not detain an employee against his or her will, either physically or through threats (such as termination or a call to the police). Unlawful detention may be accomplished by violence, threats or any means that restrain a person from moving from one place to another. You must be careful never to give the impression that the employee will be physically confined or restrained during the interview. You must always advise a witness that they have a clear option to leave the interview at any time. You should never attempt to prevent a witness from leaving the room or try to restrain the witness with threats. If the witness can show that the threat caused just fear of injury to their person, reputation or property, the company may be liable for damages.

That being said, there are consequences for the employee's decision not to submit to an interview. In many private-sector companies, this is grounds for dismissal.

## *Emotional Distress*

An employee may claim emotional distress if an aggressive investigator conducts an interview in such a way that the employee feels unusually humiliated or threatened. These claims can be successful if the action is seen as offensive to a reasonable person and would be viewed as outrageous by a reasonable society. There is generally no valid reason for an investigator or anyone else to shout at a witness, use slurs or other demeaning language, or humiliate the employee.

## *Malicious Prosecution*

Employers may be sued for malicious prosecution if they are not judicious regarding the criminal prosecution of an employee. If an employee is reported to the police and portrayed as some sort of criminal, but for some reason there turns out to be no basis for criminal charges, that employee may sue the employer for malicious prosecution. If an employee is suspected of wrongdoing, and under the circumstances it would be appropriate to get law enforcement involved, the better approach is to report to the law enforcement managers whatever the problem is and make the information available. If the information happens to include the names of employees who may have material knowledge of a crime, the company should be able to defend against such a claim. It is not malicious prosecution to simply give factual information to the police and request their assistance.

*Wrongful Discharge*

If the investigation is not conducted thoroughly, reasonably, and with conclusions supported by the facts, an employee who is dismissed based on information discovered in the investigation may subsequently file a claim of wrongful discharge. A similar result may occur if the investigation is not conducted according to your established procedures. And while a company may decide to fire an employee based on the results of an investigation, there is no guarantee that a jury, looking at the findings with the benefit of hindsight, will agree with the company's conclusions.

## B) Protecting the Findings from Disclosure

You must understand the applicable legal privileges and take affirmative action to ensure they apply to your investigations to the fullest extent possible. However, the purposes of the investigation process also include business improvement. There will also be pressures by executive management to see the fruits of the investigation. The desire to protect privileges should not override the fundamental need to use the organizational intelligence derived from the investigation process to improve the company's operations. Both the privileges and the investigation are meant to benefit the company. Moreover, the legal protection offered to investigative reports by these privileges is neither complete nor entirely predictable.

This requires a basic awareness—especially for non-lawyers—of what the privileges are, and what they do not cover. There is no ironclad way to prevent disclosure of investigative reports. Considering the broader dissemination of investigative information within companies, assume that any part of their investigations may be subject to disclosure in a lawsuit or similar proceeding.

The documents and other communications created during an investigation are not usually privileged from disclosure to government regulators, private litigants or other third parties in litigation or other legal proceedings where the investigation may be relevant. This is often true even when a company attorney is involved in your investigation. Accordingly, do not rely on the privilege when generating documents. If there is any question about whether communications during an investigation can be protected from disclosure, your legal department should be consulted to determine whether privilege can or should apply and what steps are required in that particular situation to maintain it.

Privileges can be waived if the company discloses the privileged communication (intentionally or accidentally) to a third party or, in some cases, even to people within the company who are not essential to the investigation. Once the privilege over a particular communication has been waived, it cannot be reclaimed.

Your investigation plan should set out whether the investigation is to be carried out on a privileged basis or not. Everyone involved in the investigation should know that no decision should be made to waive privileges applicable to a workplace investigation until after its conclusion. If a company decides before or during an investigation to waive an applicable privilege, it may be argued that subsequent communications are not privileged because they were not intended to be confidential. This can harm the company especially if the decision is made before potentially damaging facts are discovered in the investigation.

This section is intended only to give a brief overview of these important topics. Please consult your company's legal department for specific guidance.

## *The Attorney-Client Privilege*

A company is entitled to the protections of the attorney-client privilege. The privilege belongs solely to the corporation, not to any employee. There are several factors relevant to the availability of the attorney-client privilege in the context of a workplace investigation:

1. The communications were made by company employees under instructions from superiors in order for the company to secure legal advice from counsel;
2. The information needed by company counsel in order to formulate legal advice was not otherwise available to executive management;
3. The information communicated concerned matters within the scope of the employee's corporate duties;
4. The employees were aware that the reason for the communication with counsel was to enable the company to obtain legal advice; and
5. The communications were ordered to be kept confidential and they remain confidential.

The attorney-client privilege only protects the communication from discovery; the underlying information contained in the communication—witnesses and business documents—is discoverable. The privilege does not extend to the underlying facts.

Communications that merely transmit business-related facts may be discoverable, because the privilege most often applies to requests for legal advice. The transfer of non-privileged documents from the corporation to the attorney similarly does not make the documents privileged. Communications made for purposes other than to obtain counsel's legal advice, including communications made to third parties, are not privileged. Consequently, simply funneling communications through a lawyer will not shield an investigation from disclosure, because communications for business purposes are not privileged.

Here are some best practices you should follow when your company believes it is essential to maintain the attorney-client privilege in a particular investigation:

- The investigation should be conducted by an attorney, preferably one who has had investigatory experience.
- If outside counsel is retained, the attorney-client relation should be established expressly at the outset of any agreement between the company and outside counsel. The agreement should state plainly that the outside attorney has been engaged solely to conduct the investigation and give advice to the board of directors.
- The attorney should state explicitly to all persons who are interviewed that he is serving as the company's attorney for the purpose of providing legal advice to the company.
- Documents should be kept under control. They should be marked "privileged and confidential."
- The company's employees should be instructed not to discuss the investigation or make public statements about it. Disclosures of privileged information should be limited to those with a need to know, be narrowly defined, and be accompanied by an instruction to not reproduce privileged materials without authorization.
- When preparing written reports, keep them brief, general and evaluative.
- Ensure that interviews are summarized and include personal opinions in order to maximize the likelihood that the privilege will attach.

- Discard all unnecessary documentation generated during the investigation.

If an in-house counsel conducts the investigation, there are risks of waiving the attorney-client privilege. If the in-house counsel plays both a legal and a business role, then the in-house counsel should make a good-faith effort to make sure that all conversations and documents have a legal or a business purpose, but not a combination of both. Whether the conversation or document is legal or business should be expressly stated and documented.

If the company is concerned with an inadvertent waiver, any documentation upon which the company may need to rely on in litigation should be prepared by someone other than an in-house attorney. This would include, for example, the investigation's findings and the basis for the findings. Similarly, the decisions about what did or did not happen should not be made by the attorney but by executive management. Finally, the attorney who represents the company in any court matter should be someone other than the attorney who participated in the investigation. If the facts disclosed in the investigation formed a basis for any employment decision, the lawyer becomes a potential witness.

The application of the attorney-client privilege to an in-house attorney conducting an investigation is questionable. First, the lawyer's task as an investigator requires compiling relevant facts to form a legal opinion. This blurs the distinction between investigative and legal activities. Second, as a participant in the corporation, the distinction blurs between the lawyer's role as business advisor and the role as a legal advisor. While it is true that the suspected commission of a legal violation triggers the investigation, that may not be sufficient to cloak the investigation under the attorney-client privilege.

## *The Work-Product Doctrine*

An attorney's work product, including factual investigation in the course of an investigation, is subject to qualified protection. The objective of the privilege is to protect an attorney's trial preparation from exploitation by an adverse party in anticipation of litigation. However, in contrast to the attorney-client privilege, the work-product privilege is not as broad. An adverse party can obtain discovery of the documents if that party makes a proper application to the court.

Work product includes (i) material prepared or mental impressions developed in anticipation of litigation by or for a party or a party's representatives;

and (ii) communications made in anticipation of litigation or for trial between a party and the party's representatives, or among the parties' representatives. The doctrine protects the attorney's thought process and issue formulation. The doctrine also protects the mechanical compilation of information to the extent the compilation reveals the attorney's thought processes.

The work-product privilege is broader than the attorney-client privilege because the work-product privilege protects communications with non-attorneys. But the work-product privilege is narrower in that the communication must be in anticipation of litigation or in preparation for trial.

For the work-product privilege to apply, litigation need not be imminent, but the documents must have been prepared because of the prospect of litigation. However, documents prepared in the ordinary course of business do fall outside the scope of the work-product privilege, even if litigation is imminent.

The work-product privilege distinguishes between "fact" work product and "opinion" work product. The former means work product that reflects certain facts, rather than mental impressions. This type of work product can be discovered when a judge decides there is a substantial need and to avoid undue hardship. Lawyers conducting investigations should ensure that their mental impressions are included wherever possible in all written materials.

Opinion work product is generally regarded as non-discoverable. Therefore, attorneys taking notes during employee interviews should intersperse those notes with evaluations of the witness's candor and the attorney's legal theories appropriate to the facts observed. Adverse parties may not obtain documents that contain the mental impressions, conclusions, opinions or legal theories of any attorney concerning litigation. Also, while factual data is not ordinarily protected from discovery, where documents are assembled by or at a lawyer's direction in anticipation of litigation, discovery may be precluded to prevent revealing the lawyer's thought processes.

### The Self-Evaluative Privilege

The attorney-client privilege and work-product privilege do not protect materials that are not communications for the purpose of obtaining legal advice or that are not prepared in anticipation of litigation. Reports and other documents that may be intended to be confidential are frequently discoverable in litigation.

In some court jurisdictions, however, there is a recognized privilege for self-critical analysis on public policy grounds. The rationale behind this privilege is consistent with that favoring protection of workplace investigative reports from disclosure. Those jurisdictions apparently wish to encourage companies and other entities to internally examine their operations and to improve them. Documents protected under this privilege have satisfied each of these criteria: (i) the report was the result of a critical self-analysis by the party seeking the protection; (ii) the public has a strong interest in maintaining the free flow of information of the kind sought; and (iii) the information is of the type whose flow would be stifled without protection. To these requirements should be added the general proviso that no document will be privileged unless it was prepared with the expectation that it would be kept confidential, and that it has in fact been kept confidential.

The majority of federal courts have refused to recognize the privilege when presented in any context, especially when the information sought is factual rather than analytical or evaluative information. Ultimately, the decision as to the level of documentation carried out during the investigation process is one for each company to make independently, based on the company's own circumstances.

> **Process Pointer:** For all intents, the legal privileges do not to protect the investigation documents—including final reports and memos—from disclosure in a lawsuit or prosecution. Additionally, the facts stated in investigation documents come from other sources, such as witnesses and documents that could be obtained directly from those sources. So make the investigation documents professional and objectively complete. Never write anything on paper that you would not be comfortable explaining in a courtroom.

## C) Referrals to Law Enforcement

Some of your investigations will conclude that the company was the victim of a crime. Your findings will present management with three options: reporting the matter to the police—local, state, or federal law enforcement managers—for possible prosecution, filing a civil lawsuit, and/or pursuing claims against third parties and their insurers.

If your company is typical, when some crime is suspected, your executives want the police to swoop down, make some arrests, and cart the bad guys off to jail. However, if executive management wants to report the matter to the police for possible criminal action against the wrongdoers, they must be counseled carefully. The company must consider the benefits and risks of contacting the police.

### *Business Goals*

The referral of the matter to the police should never be simply a knee-jerk reaction. The referral must further a business purpose. You must, therefore, identify the company's goal in referring the matter to the police. Does the company simply want the satisfaction of having reported it to the police, regardless of what happens after the report is made? (This can be useful if the company wants to publicize it internally as a deterrent to others.) Would simply the arrest of the wrongdoer be sufficient, regardless of whether he is convicted? Does the company want the wrongdoers punished or to send a public message to its marketplace? The company must make this decision at the outset because it affects the internal preparation of the referral and the amount of resources the company should expect to devote later on to achieve its desired result.

### *The Company's Reputation*

Although executive management may feel that they are vindicating the company's rights by contacting the police, it is nonetheless a public act. If the wrongdoing was enabled by some internal business failure, the company will be announcing that failure to its customers and competitors. The company may also be saying, however indirectly and unintentionally, that it has hired dishonest people. This may lead to questions by shareholders and the marketplace about the competence of management to supervise employees adequately.

On the other hand, your company may view the referral as an act of institutional hygiene, and find that it shows the company is committed to the highest ethical standards. (It may also highlight the effectiveness of your company's compliance program.) The referral shows that compliance-minded senior managers "walk the talk."

The important point is to consider fully the varying perceptions the referral will have.

## *Contacting an Agency*

Now that executive management has decided to report the matter to the police, which agency do you contact? Naturally, you want the best agency to handle your case. Remember, however, that your choice may be among a number of law enforcement agencies with jurisdiction. Federal criminal laws cover most of the common misconduct committed by company employees, including various types of fraud, interstate transport of stolen property, commercial bribery, intellectual property crimes, and racketeering. State criminal laws cover most of the same conduct. Therefore, a criminal act that can be prosecuted by federal authorities may also be prosecuted by state or local ones.

Take the time to choose the right one in light of the nature of the crime, its complexity, the dollar amounts involved, and the location of the incident. Although your executive management may feel comforted to know that a high-profile agency like the FBI or Secret Service has the case, a referral to local police, while less glamorous, might produce a faster and more meaningful result.

However, do not shop your case around to a number of agencies. One of the first questions you will be asked when the report is taken is whether any other agency has been contacted. Whether for reasons of resources or turf, many agencies do not take a case that another agency is handling, even if that other agency has only taken nominal steps. This is also why the decision to contact the police and the initial contact must be coordinated by executive management. A well-intentioned manager who called the police to make a report when he first suspected wrongdoing may prevent you from having any other agency—especially a more appropriate agency—take the case later.

## *Timing*

Time your initial contact properly. Do not contact the police prematurely. The police cannot investigate every allegation, so wait until you have developed sufficient facts to explain—and document—what happened.

Remember, of course, that the investigation will only be one matter that competes for their resources. Their world is a fluid one, and it is full of unexpected shifts in resources. Business-related investigations often give way to more urgent police matters. Police detectives and government agents are usually busy, with other matters under investigation and prosecution. Unless the magnitude of the misconduct is such that it is deemed a priority, the investigation will proceed as resources allow, and that may mean waiting for an extended period of time.

## *Sympathy*

You must make your company appear sympathetic. Police and prosecutors deal on a daily basis with violent crimes and other inhumanity. Those victims motivate the authorities. The authorities, in contrast, may view the crime you report as the result of poor business practices that created the opportunity for the problem rather than seeing the company as someone's victim. This is where the importance of emphasizing your compliance program comes in. An effective program shows that the company takes proactive measures to ensure that the company and its employees act ethically, and that the company has affirmatively prohibited the conduct in question. Your company may then be perceived as having been victimized despite its own efforts to protect itself.

## *Case Complexity*

When you get the opportunity to present what your workplace investigation found, don't make your case appear too complex. Be able to summarize your findings in one sentence. Otherwise, there is little realistic hope that it will be meaningfully investigated.

The police deal with serious crimes on a daily basis. It is relatively easy for them to assemble the evidence to prove, for example, the elements of a robbery. This is their world. The corporate world, with its policies, internal processes and nomenclature, compliance processes, hierarchies and business groups, is not that familiar to them.

Don't expect the police to embrace the complexity of your business operations as an opportunity for them to expand their knowledge. Most lack a business background, and they may not readily confess to you that they do not understand the machinations of how you do business. Consequently, authorities may focus on what is familiar to them and ignore your report.

Be prepared to overcome their reluctance. One way to do this is by "gift-wrapping" the investigation. Marshal the known facts into an objective report. Organize copies of key documents. Document the chain of custody for them. Build a paper-trail or chronology of what you believe happened. Provide a list of witnesses. Offer an expert witness from your company, if necessary. Prepare charts, graphs, maps or other demonstrative aids. Be prepared to break down the incident into simple terms that a layman could follow. Also, be prepared to identify potential problems or factual gaps. The more complete and documented your package of information, the more likely it is to be prosecuted. Present the case to the police personally, not over the telephone. This will demonstrate your company's commitment to the process.

## *Cooperation*

Be prepared to cooperate fully. Although you may not always have the opportunity, depending on the agency, you should try to expand your role from that of a victim to being part of the investigative team.

Assign a single point of contact to facilitate all company-related inquiries and to ensure quick access to people, documents and information. Offer to be a company translator, guide and intermediary for the police. Get senior managers involved to show their commitment. Most importantly, remember that the police and prosecutors will approach the case in terms of probable cause and burdens of proof. Everything you do that helps them to address those factors lessens the chances that your case will not be prosecuted.

However, be prepared to surrender all control over the investigation after the referral. Police and prosecutors control their investigations. They may also insist that the company take no further action on its own to avoid compromising a possible criminal prosecution.

For some significant investigations, you should also recognize that the criminal investigation may disrupt operations. The police may need access to computer systems, employees, and business records. Your investigation, however comprehensive, does not prevent the police from making their own inquiries, and they likely will anyway.

## *Prosecutor Resources*

The police will usually use the information you give them and make their own additional inquiries. If this confirms a crime has occurred, the evidence is usually presented to a prosecutor. This is a crucial step in the process.

Any police agency will take a report of possible criminal activity. Your goal is the prosecution of the wrongdoers.

You must focus on what it takes to capture the prosecutor's interest in prosecuting the wrongdoers. This may not be easy. For example, due to demands of police, prosecutors fail to pursue 75 percent of bank check fraud cases. According to the U.S. Government Accountability Office, in large cities where a majority of resources are used to prosecute violent crime, the percentage rises to 90 percent.

A prosecutor has broad discretion to decide not to prosecute, even if the company and the police believe the case is a compelling one. You should accept this reality and help build a case that (i) would be attractive to a jury, (ii) would present the company as a sympathetic victim, and (iii) has sufficient proof to justify a verdict beyond a reasonable doubt. Don't be afraid to use some salesmanship. If your case has some hook to catch the prosecutor's interest—dollar amount, organized-crime involvement, headline-grabbing facts—be sure to emphasize it.

The government has different objectives than your company. They are focused on righting the wrongs against society, not the wrong done to your company. Your company's goal could be sidelined by plea bargains, cooperating testimony, and political factors. External factors, such as national-security demands on federal agencies, may also affect the results your company seeks. Finally, the prosecutor may make decisions about charging, settlement or strategy with which the company may not agree.

### *Be Realistic*

Be prepared to temper management expectations. Managers should be educated on the realistic outcome of the referral. Their likely vision of someone being led out in handcuffs—known as the "perp walk"—will rarely occur. The time needed for these prosecutions will not usually be as quick as management would like. Minor offenses may not be severely punished, and jail time may not be likely. Senior managers must understand that a referral may neither bring a prompt resolution of the matter nor will it necessarily bring prompt restitution. There is just no "magic bullet" to help a company that is victimized by crime.

In most cases, contacting the police should be used as a last resort when other options will not work. And it should never be considered as just another step in your company's incident-management process. Better to solve your business problem first. The police can be contacted if the company then wants to seek a prosecution. And if executive management fully supports the referral and appreciates its benefits and risks, your efforts may be worth it.

## *Criminal Recovery and Restitution*

The criminal courts provide for victim restitution, and this result is frequently ordered as an attempt to make the victim whole. In reality, this is ineffective for your company. Few defendants every pay all or most of the restitution they have been ordered to pay.

Do not look to the criminal courts to recover from those who steal or commit fraud against your company. You are asking for disappointment. Do not recommend your company's leadership make the criminal court system part of your recovery strategy.

> **Process Pointer:** When you involve law enforcement in any investigation, you decrease your chances of a successful resolution and double the cost of the investigation. Because the company now loses control of the decision-making, the investigation will be drawn out to meet the goals of the police and the prosecutor.

# APPENDIX A

## Selling the Value of Workplace Investigations to Management

Before you can sell the business leaders on an improved approach to investigations, you will need to have a good professional relationship with them. There are many ways to build good relationships with senior managers. Some of them include:

- Respect their legitimate business objectives and redefine your success to include the achievement of those objectives.
- Respect their limited resources by delivering value and properly managing their expectations.
- Respect their decisions to take calculated risks in running the business.
- Respect the fact that you are assisting the executives to run their business, and they are entitled to direct the battle plan.
- Build trust with senior executives. This influences your credibility and determines whether your message is convincing or not.

There are also some key selling points to use in soliciting the support of the executive management.

### *Return on Investment*

Like other business functions, the workplace investigations process should have a measurable return on investment ("ROI"). A properly engineered investigation produces tangible results, such as the recovery of money, the termination of dishonest employees, and prosecution of wrongdoers. The more substantive the ROI, the more likely the process will be embraced by the company and receive the funding it deserves.

Traditionally, investigations return value to the company by:

- Stopping financial losses;
- Changing processes and procedures to improve operations;
- Increasing productivity;
- Obtaining restitution or concessions from wrongdoers.

The financial impact of a successful investigation is important to recognize. For example, if your company's EBITDA (earnings before interest, taxes, depreciation and amortization) is ten percent, your company has to generate $10 in revenue for every dollar it pays out in losses. Conversely, every dollar recovered through a successful investigation equals $10 in revenue your company did not have to generate.

> **Process Pointer:** EBITDA—that's speaking their language. Develop a payout example using your company's financial data to show the value you bring (as well as the cost for doing nothing).

### Risk Management

Running a business is all about taking smart risks and calculated risks. But not all risks are created equal. Proper risk management includes the ability to recognize potential hot spots. This leads to better decision making regarding how much risk the company wants to reduce, transfer or avoid. It allows executive management to manage problems when they are still small and relatively inexpensive to deal with. Investigations are valuable components of a company's efforts to identify systematically the risks to the business and to ensure that appropriate processes commensurate with the risks are implemented.

Although they focus on specific allegations against past conduct, investigations actually provide some foresight. If the investigation findings are seriously considered and gleaned for "lessons learned," the findings will offer insights into how similar problems may be occurring elsewhere and in the future.

In risk-management terms, investigations identify existing sources of revenue loss and prevent further losses. Investigations shield the company from liability or help reduce it. Your company may become aware of problems or practices that could expose the company to criminal liability, civil lawsuits or sanctions. Identifying and repairing these problems before a possible outside investigation begins can give the company the opportunity to take remedial measures, comply with relevant laws or regulatory standards, or eliminate other problems that were previously unknown to management. Finally, aggregate workplace-investigation data can be presented to show risk trends of certain employee behaviors, troubled management, or business regions.

> **Process Pointer:** Most misconduct is the result of a combination of factors: an opportunistic person enabled by poor business practices. This is why risk identification is an important part of any investigation. When you have the choice between incompetence and intentional wrongdoing, don't rush to believe that the misconduct happened in a factual vacuum.

When seen this way, investigations avoid future costs. When conducted in-house, the transactional cost of an investigation is minimal. They offer value to business because they connect investigations with financial and operational policies and procedures. Timely and meaningful findings avoid damage to reputation and investor confidence. They protect the stock price. They avoid the personal liability of directors and officers. They avoid civil litigation and criminal penalties. On a practical level, a thorough investigation may even help the dispute-resolution process of company claims by identifying the strengths and weaknesses of your company's position.

Ask yourself how to calculate the value-added of a properly conducted investigation when senior executives consider these questions:

- How much could be lost if the risk is not managed intelligently?
- What is the company's vulnerability to the risk?
- Is the risk correlated with other risk exposures?
- If some think the risk is minimal, how can we get assurance that the confidence is justified?
- How much will it cost to manage the risk?
- Is there a potential reputation risk impact from the risk?

In a perfect corporate world, executive management partners with you to identify and prioritize business risks. This gives the executive management a stake in your group and maximizes the value of investigations to the business.

Proper risk management gives the company some competitive benefits:

- Improved ability to prevent, quickly detect, correct, and escalate critical risk issues;
- Reduced burden on business operations;

- Reduced costs by improved sharing of information and integration of risk-management functions;
- Improved strategic flexibility for both upside and downside scenarios;
- The ability to provide a comfort level to the board of directors and executive management that the full range of risks is understood and managed.
- Good marketing makes the investigation process an essential part of that value proposition.

### *Good Corporate Citizenship*

Companies want to be perceived publicly as good corporate citizens. Corporations generally want to be recognized in the relevant community as a contributor to shared values through the creation of jobs, income to the community and the payment of taxes. To the extent that the corporation can build a constituency beyond the shareholders, the greater the likelihood that company senior managers will see the benefits of an effective workplace investigations process. But don't forget that, unless tied in with business-oriented goals, this public-service message will be ignored as just another appeal to a business senior manager's conscience, with predictable results.

> **Process Pointer:** Never presume that you care more about the company than your colleagues in other departments. It is likely that their efforts, rather than yours, drive the revenue into the company that pays everyone's salaries. Also, the "moral high ground" is an off-putting message. Be careful with the ethics messages. These messages should be used only to complement the business justifications for the process.

### *Projecting a Strong Public Image*

Attention to ethics is good public relations. The fact that a company regularly gives attention to its ethics portrays a strong positive to the public. People see those companies as valuing people more than profit, as striving to operate with the utmost of integrity and honor. Aligning behavior with values is critical to effective marketing and public relations programs.

## Stakeholder Expectations

Investigations that identify misconduct serve your company's broader interests by helping the company meet the expectations of the business' internal and external stakeholders. (A stakeholder could be the company's employees, shareholders, government agencies or outside groups.) A business that incorporates ethical principles into its operations will likely fare better in the market. If an ethical lapse then occurs in the future, the risk of adverse publicity will be less as the public may see it as an aberration in the company's otherwise clean image.

## Quality Control

Properly conducted investigations are a form of organizational intelligence, provided that the focus is not limited to the simple question of whether misconduct actually occurred. Information gleaned from an investigation improves business operations by identifying deficiencies in operations. When done well, investigations offer executive management each of the following:

- The company values, ethics and expected behaviors are communicated to employees through the conduct of the investigation and the application of a code of conduct.
- Key business risks are identified and assessed.
- Information can be reported to management, the board and stakeholders in an accurate, timely and reliable way.
- The company's true culture can be measured, as well as the need for additional training or better management supervision.

> **Process Pointer:** Experience is the best teacher. You can expect that an incident that has occurred will occur again if the underlying causes have not been corrected.

## The Tip of the Iceberg Concern

It seems reasonable to believe that most employees report only a fraction of their concerns and allegations to the attention of the compliance department. As a result, complaints of possible or actual misconduct must be taken seriously.

Each complaint is important in its own right. Each complaint may also reflect similar concerns held, but unexpressed, by other people. Companies should take all the feedback they can get as opportunities to learn how processes may work more effectively and efficiently.

## *Business Counseling*

Your investigation findings need not only speak for themselves. Offer your value to the business. Become fully integrated into the functioning of your company (or the business divisions you serve). Become an active participant in meetings and ask questions. This enables you to appreciate the issues that the company faces and get to know the political dynamics within your company. The better you understand the business leaders, the better you can advise them. The more you can advise them, the more valuable you and the group will be perceived.

# APPENDIX B

## Compliance & Ethics Issue Reporting and Response Policy

1. **Applicability and Responsibility**

    (a) This Policy applies to all employees of the company and replaces all previous policies concerning this subject.

    (b) Each employee and agent is responsible for ensuring that his or her actions comply with this Policy. Each manager is responsible for his or her department's compliance and for informing his or her employees and agents about this Policy.

2. **Basis and Object**

    (a) This Policy specifies the manner in which the company shall report, receive, retain and respond to compliance and ethics issues, including, but not limited to, the company's accounting, accounting controls and auditing matters, that are reported by colleagues, associates or others. This Policy also strictly prohibits discharging, harassing, discriminating or taking any adverse action against any employee or agent in the terms and conditions of employment because of any lawful act done to provide information to assist in a company or government investigation or proceeding involving an alleged violation of law or company policy.

    (b) This Policy is mandatory for all employees.

    (c) The purpose of this Policy is to comply with all applicable legal requirements regarding the reporting, receipt, retention, and response to compliance and ethics issues including, without limitation, those matters arising under the "Code of Conduct" in the company. The focus shall be on business and professional standards of conduct, compliance with applicable law, good corporate citizenship, prevention and detection of misconduct, and the identification of areas of particular risk to the company.

(d) The purpose of this Policy is also to facilitate the measurement and reporting of reported incidents of possible compliance or ethics-related misconduct on a company-wide basis to the Corporate Governance Committee and the Audit Committee of the Board of Directors.

3. **Definitions and Explanations**

   (a) By using the term "Misconduct," we mean any fraud or violation of law, company policy, procedure or ethical standard of conduct by the company or any of its employees or agents. Misconduct includes each of the categories of personal conduct described in the appendix to this Policy.

   (b) By using the term "the company," we mean all legal entities/business groups that are part of _____ and their respective employees and agents.

   (c) By using the term "Ethics Office," we mean the company's Corporate compliance department.

   (d) By using the term "the company officer," we mean any CEO, CFO, COO, General Counsel, and other such senior manager officers, senior financial officers or other members of the senior company management.

   (e) By using the term "Guide to Conducting an Investigation," we mean the guidance document issued by the Ethics Office setting forth the procedures to be followed in investigating allegations of Misconduct.

   (f) By using the term "the company agents," we mean all non-employees of the company who are properly authorized to act on the company's behalf.

(g) By using the term "the company Compliance & Ethics Line," we mean the reporting system with which the company has contracted with a third party to provide a mechanism to confidentially and anonymously report any observed or suspected instances of Misconduct. The company Compliance & Ethics Line is available to call, toll free, 24 hours a day, seven days a week and can take calls in almost any language at the following telephone numbers:
- **United States & Canada:**
- **Outside the United States & Canada:**
  (Country Access Number)

The company Compliance & Ethics Line can also be contacted on the Internet at www._____.com.

(h) By using the term "Report," we mean an incident of actual or suspected Misconduct that is reported to a manager, an appropriate department head, Internal Audit, the Legal Department, Human Resources Department, the Ethics Office, the Board of Directors or the company Compliance & Ethics Line.

4. **Procedures, Rules and Guidelines**
   (a) Responsibility for Reporting Misconduct:
   - All the company employees and the company agents are obligated to report any observed instances of Misconduct to either their manager, an appropriate department head, Internal Audit, the Legal Department, Human Resources Department, the Ethics Office, the Board of Directors or the company Compliance & Ethics Line.

   - Once reported, the manager, department head, Internal Audit, the Legal Department, and/or Human Resources Department shall take all necessary steps to ensure that the Ethics Office has been informed of the Report, regardless of the manner in which the report shall be investigated. This is to allow the Ethics Office to track these reports centrally for the company. The Ethics Office and other key internal departments shall establish a process by which the Ethics Office shall be effectively and expeditiously informed.

- The Ethics Office shall establish and administer a process by which other key internal departments shall be notified of the receipt by the Ethics Office of a Report. That department may, at its election, appropriately participate in the investigation.

- The Ethics Office shall ensure that the process by which Reports are taken, processed, investigated and reported complies with local law and regulation in the jurisdiction where a Report is made.

(b) Response to Reports of Misconduct
- The Ethics Office has primary responsibility to ensure that a detailed, competent and appropriate investigation of the Report has occurred.

- The Ethics Office shall either perform, or arrange for, a professional, independent and objective investigation. The resources devoted to such investigations should be proportionate to the nature of the Report. The Ethics Office should use the resources available in the Legal Department, Human Resources Department, or Internal Audit as appropriate, to ensure the independence and objectivity of all investigations of Reports.

- The Ethics Office shall ensure that the company employees who investigate Reports are competent and adequately trained for that purpose. The Ethics Office shall provide or arrange for such training when needed. The Ethics Office shall also ensure that the investigation process is consistently applied throughout the company.

- The purposes of an investigation of a Report shall include (i) to determine if the specific allegation(s) of Misconduct are substantiated by the facts elicited, (ii) to determine whether other Misconduct may have occurred, (iii) to identify areas of potential risk (financial or legal) to the company as a result of the Misconduct, and (iv) to identify areas of business operations that may require improvement as a result of the Misconduct. The Ethics Office shall have the discretion to determine the appropriate scope of an investigation.

- Once an investigation is completed and findings are made, the Ethics Office or investigator shall (i) provide appropriate feedback to the person or persons who made the Report regarding the outcome of the investigation; (ii) advise the responsible management as to the specific facts determined by the investigation to allow management to take actions, as may be appropriate in the circumstances, to discipline any company employees who engaged in Misconduct. The Ethics Office should also recommend any needed improvements in policies and procedures to avoid repetition of the Misconduct.

- The investigation shall be conducted according to the protocols specified in the Guide to Conducting an Investigation.
- All allegations of Misconduct regarding any company officer who is not a member of the Ethics Office shall be immediately forwarded to the Ethics Office for investigation. The Ethics Office shall have responsibility for performing or overseeing any investigation regarding the alleged Misconduct of such the company officers to ensure independence and objectivity.

- All allegations of Misconduct by the members of the Ethics Office shall be immediately forwarded to the Corporate Governance Committee of the Board of Directors who shall have responsibility for overseeing all investigations regarding the alleged Misconduct of the members of the Ethics Office to ensure independence and objectivity.

- All Reports received by the Ethics Office (and associated investigation findings) shall be recorded by the Ethics Office in its Report database. This information, whether on an aggregate or investigation-specific basis, shall be made appropriately available to other departments and the company's auditors.

- The Ethics Office shall take all necessary steps to protect from unnecessary disclosure the confidentiality, sensitivity and applicable legal protections for this information. The identity of a company employee or a company agent who has made a Report shall be protected to the extent possible, consistent with this Policy and applicable law.

(c) Periodic Summary Reports and Evaluation
- The Ethics Office shall summarize and periodically report to the company executive management and the Corporate Governance and Audit Committee of the Board of Directors information regarding Reports and the company's response thereto with regard to matters that are reported to the Ethics Office.

- The Ethics Office shall work with executive management to evaluate instances of Misconduct and determine whether changes to policies, procedures, training, monitoring, audits, control systems or other steps must be taken to prevent or reduce the possibility of such Misconduct occurring in the future.

(d) Contacting the Board of Directors
- Employees, investors or other interested parties may report instances of Misconduct directly to the Board of Directors by either calling one of the telephone numbers or writing to the address provided below:
    - If calling from inside the United States or Canada, dial (800) _____.

- If calling from outside of the United States or Canada, dial the AT&T Country Access Number, then, when prompted, dial (800) _____.

(Note: Those calling from outside the United States or Canada can obtain their country AT&T Access Number by logging on to: www.usa.att.com/traveler/index.jsp.)

Correspondence to the Board of Directors should be mailed to:
The company Board of Directors Helpline

_____
_____
_____

- Calls and written correspondence made to the Board of Directors via the phone numbers or address provided above shall be received 24 hours a day, seven days a week by a third party service provider with whom the company has contracted to receive such messages on the company's behalf. When the service provider receives either a telephone call or written correspondence directed to one or more of the company's directors, the service provider shall fax correspondence and email call reports to the company's Chief Senior Manager Officer, Chief Financial Officer, Group Chief Compliance and Business Ethics Officer and General Counsel. These corporate officers shall then review the written correspondence and call reports to facilitate the delivery of such correspondence to the company's Directors and to recommend, what if, any action should be taken in response to the correspondence or call reports.

- All call reports or correspondence shall be forwarded to the intended board member(s) unless they are of a trivial nature or otherwise not related to accounting, internal controls, auditing matters, corporate governance, safety, health or environmental issues or any other significant legal or ethical issues at the company. However, a report shall be made to the Corporate Governance Committee and Audit Committee of any correspondence not forwarded to the Board of Directors, and all such reports and correspondence shall be preserved and made available to any Directors who wish to review it.

5. **Retaliation**

The company employees and the company agents are strictly prohibited from discharging, harassing, discriminating or taking any adverse action against any employee in the terms and conditions of employment because of (i) the employee takes any lawful action done to provide information to assist in a company or government investigation or proceeding involving alleged Misconduct; or (ii) the employee made a Report honestly and in good faith. However, this provision should not be interpreted as protecting the company employee from disciplinary action resulting from his or her own Misconduct.

6. **Record Keeping**

Records of all investigations of Misconduct by the company employees and the company agents are considered confidential and shall be maintained in a secure location for a minimum of ten years from the date of the Report, after which the information may be destroyed unless it is relevant to any pending or potential litigation, inquiry, or investigation, in which case the information may not be destroyed and must be retained for the duration of that litigation inquiry, or investigation and thereafter as necessary.

7. **Controlling / Monitoring**
   (a) Unless otherwise specified in this Policy, it is the responsibility of each local manager, department head and the Ethics Office to set up the necessary controls and processes to ensure the accurate respect of this Policy.

(b) The adherence of the procedures established in this Policy shall be supervised and monitored by the Ethics Office on a regular basis.

8. **Violations - Reporting and Sanctioning**
    (a) Any violation of this Policy must be reported to the Ethics Office or the company Compliance & Ethics Line.

    (b) Violations of this Policy will result in disciplinary action up to and including termination of employment with the company.

9. **Approval / Amendments**
    (a) This Policy, as amended, is approved by the Corporate Governance Committee and the Audit Committee of the company at its meeting of _____. This Policy enters into force on _____.

    (b) Amendments to this Policy are only to be made by the Corporate Governance Committee and the Audit Committee of the company.

10. **Appendix**

Reports of Misconduct relate to the following types of personal conduct by a company employee or a company agent:

**Abuse of Ethics or other Hotline:** the bad-faith use of the company Compliance & Ethics Line or other reporting processes to harass a company employee or the company agent or to file knowingly false information.

**Competitive Issues:** improper sales and marketing practices. This category includes allegations of unfair competition, unethical marketing practices, using a competitor's trade secrets, and making disparaging comments about competitors. An allegation of "unfair competition" includes discussing prices, strategies or sales terms with competitors. It also includes agreements covering customers or territories. This category also includes obtaining information about a competitor in some improper way.

**Conflicts of Interest:** a company employee or the company agent made a decision while allowing their personal loyalties to conflict or appear to conflict with the company's interests. This category includes hiring or supervising a relative, having a financial, business or personal interest in a company vendor or competitor, or having some outside personal interest that conflicts with the company's interests. This includes outside employment that creates a conflict of interest or diminishes productivity and effectiveness.

**Confidential or Proprietary Information Issues:** a company employee or the company agent improperly lost, used or possessed non-public information which the company is required to safeguard. This category includes software piracy, improper data copying, and the unauthorized use of a company employee or the company agent's patent, copyright and trademark rights. This category includes the improper disclosure of the company business plans, pricing data, marketing programs, personnel information, and financial reports. This category also includes client-related confidential information.

**Customer-site Incident:** a company employee or the company agent acted improperly at a customer location. This category includes on-site illegal activity, theft, vandalism and physical violence.

**Employment Practice Issues:** a company employee or the company agent acted improperly in the recruiting, hiring, assignment, evaluation, promotion, training, discipline or compensation of an employee. This category includes allegations of discrimination (race, color, gender, national origin, age, marital status, religion, disability, sexual orientation, veteran status or other status protected by applicable law).

**Fraud:** the improper accounting of business transactions, or not following internal accounting and financial-reporting rules, including (i) falsifying or forging financial records; (ii) the misstatement of expenses, revenues or business transactions; (iii) fraud or deliberate error in the preparation, review or audit of internal financial reports or statutory accounts; (iv) fraud or deliberate error in the recording and maintenance of the financial and corporate records of the company; (v) false statements to investors, regulators, government managers or members of the investing public; (vi) non-compliance with the company's internal accounting controls, or other policies or procedures; (vii) misappropriation of the company assets, unlawful conduct toward employees in the workplace, violation of antitrust, anti-corruption, privacy or intellectual property laws; (viii) employee benefits fraud; (ix) corruption (i.e. bribery, extortion, kickbacks); (x) asset misappropriation (e.g., theft of the company assets, ghost employees, overstated expenses); and (xi) fraudulent statements (e.g., false employment credentials, false time records, false financial documentation).

**Gifts, Gratuities and Entertainment:** a company employee or the company agent accepted something valuable, such as a gift, tickets or entertainment, from anyone who is trying to influence a business decision. The valuable item could be offered by a supplier, customer, supervisor or subordinate, or where the employee solicited the gift, ticket or entertainment. This includes instances where the gift-giver could seek or receive special favors from the colleague. This also includes entertainment that is not for bona fide business reasons.

**Insider Trading and Securities Violations:** a company employee or the company agent knew non-public, material, the company-related information and then used that information in a stock transaction. "Non-public, material, the company-related information" includes financial results, earnings estimates, changes in management, major contract awards and potential acquisitions.

**Internal Business Operations Issues:** some activity that conflicts with established company business policies, procedures and practices. This category covers allegations that a company employee or company agent did not follow internal manuals, standard business practices or workplace health and safety procedures.

**Internal Workplace Conduct Issues:** a company employee or company agent behaved improperly while on the company premises. This category includes harassment, threats, theft of property, offensive speech, improper employee relationships, and physical violence. This includes improper soliciting and distribution of material.

**International Trade Control Issues:** improper actions in doing business outside the Home Country. ("Home Country" means the country in which the reported incident occurs.) This category includes problems with export licenses, financial transactions, anti-boycott laws, offering or making improper payments to officials outside the Home Country.

**Misuse of Internal Systems:** a company employee or the company agent improperly used the company's telephone systems, computers, e-mail, voice mail, fax machines, teleconferencing services, copiers, internal data systems, or the Internet. This includes using the systems to send illegal, sexually explicit, abusive, offensive or profane messages. This also includes improperly uploading or downloading information. This also includes using the systems for soliciting funds or distributing information that is unrelated to the company business.

**Money Laundering:** a company employee or the company agent, such as a vendor, tried to "launder" the proceeds of a crime—such as narcotics trafficking, bribery or fraud—in order to hide the money or make the amounts appear legitimate by making it look like a normal business transaction with the company.

**Political and Charitable Activity Issues:** a company employee or the company agent made a payment to a political party, political organization, charity or an elected official that directly affects the company's business interests. This category includes participating in the activities of these organizations.

**Purchasing Issues:** allegation relating to buying supplies or services for the company use. These allegations relate to how a vendor was chosen, the vendor's qualifications, or the price we were charged for the supplies or services.

**Records and Document Retention Issues:** a company employee or the company agent did not retain or safeguard the company books and records according to the company's document-retention guidelines. This category applies to the retention or destruction of the company documents in any form. This category includes destroying or concealing documents in order to avoid retention obligations.

**Regulatory Noncompliance:** a company employee or the company agent did not follow a government rule or regulation. These rules and regulations include employee-verification requirements, visa and immigration rules, payroll and tax obligations, wage/ hour laws, labor-law violations, stock-exchange and other government rules.

**Retaliation of Whistleblowers:** a company employee or the company agent who reported a possible ethics or compliance-related violation was treated unfairly because he made the report.

**Substance Abuse:** a company employee or the company agent misused alcohol or drugs (legal or illegal) while at work. This category includes a company employee or the company agent using prescription medication if that medication impaired that person's ability to do his or her job properly.

# APPENDIX C

## Sample Mission Statement

The mission of the Workplace Investigations Unit (the "WIU") is to provide the executive management of the company with a variety of coordinated investigation services. The goal of these services is to aid in accomplishing the WIU's primary purpose—improving the quality, efficiency and profitability of business processes.

It is the responsibility of the WIU to manage its investigations and the company's investigation processes in an environment that respects and enforces proper conduct by employees. This allows for the appropriate correction of employee behavior that is not consistent with our values or policies.

Misconduct by these employees is vigorously investigated. This creates confidence among employees that their concerns will be taken seriously. The WIU coordinates these investigations to ensure that group resources are used efficiently and productively.

The WIU is available to consult with other internal departments that are conducting employee-related investigations.

The WIU develops information regarding the identification of business risks and where business processes should be improved. This information is shared with key internal departments and executive management to help ensure that our customers receive the best possible services from the company.

The WIU is designated as the company's liaison with law-enforcement agencies in investigative and misconduct matters.

# APPENDIX D

## Notification Matrix for Key Internal Departments

As part of the company's commitment to an ethical workplace and to ensure that the company meets its legal obligations, the company requires colleagues and associates to report possible violations of the company Code of Conduct. The company, through the Corporate Compliance Department ("Compliance"), responds to these reports. Compliance also tracks these incidents and reports them to the Board of Directors.

Compliance has primary responsibility to ensure that a detailed investigation of any possible misconduct has occurred. Compliance, therefore, depends on its colleagues in key internal departments to notify our group when these matters arise. These notifications are essential to allow Compliance to track the incident.

This matrix facilitates appropriate communication and interaction among the key internal departments that handle compliance-related matters. Each group, depending on the report, has an interest in the incident reported, its investigation, and its outcome. Proper implementation of the matrix ensures that each of these stakeholder groups learns about an incident when it arises.

The matrix is intended only to ensure appropriate notification. The matrix does not replace a business group's existing procedures for investigating these incidents. The matrix will allow our group to collaborate in investigations when it is appropriate for us to do so.

This matrix applies to possible ethics and compliance-related violations committed by the company directors and officers, colleagues, associates, and franchisees around the world. This matrix also applies to consultants, agents and independent vendors when they act on behalf of the company.

The matrix follows this cover page and includes a glossary of terms. An "X" means that Compliance will notify this business group, if the business group is not already aware, once Compliance is notified that the incident has occurred.

# Notification Matrix for Key Internal Departments

| Reported Incident | Business Unit |
| --- | --- |
| Abuse of Ethics or Other Hotline | X |
| Abuse or Fraud of the Company Benefits | X |
| Accounting Irregularities | X |
| Branch Financial Violations | X |
| Competitive Issues | X |
| Conflicts of Interest | X |
| Confidential or Proprietary Information Issues | X |
| Customer-site Incident | X |
| Employment Practice Issues | X |
| Fraud | X |
| Gifts, Gratuities and Entertainment | X |
| Insider Trading and Securities Violations | X |
| Internal Business Operation Issues | X |
| Internal Workplace Conduct Issues | X |
| International Trade Control Issues | X |
| Kickbacks and Bribery | X |
| Misuse of Internal Systems | X |
| Money Laundering | X |
| Political and Charitable Activity Issues | X |
| Purchasing Issues | X |
| Records and Document Retention Issues | X |
| Regulatory Noncompliance | X |
| Requests for Advice or Clarification (ethics issues only) | X |
| Requests for Assistance (employee-specific issues) | X |
| Retaliation of Whistleblowers | X |
| Substance Abuse | X |

| Senior Manager | Legal | Human Resources | Compliance |
|---|---|---|---|
| X | X |   | X |
|   | X |   | X |
| X | X |   | X |
| X |   |   | X |
|   | X |   | X |
|   | X |   | X |
|   | X |   | X |
| X | X | X | X |
|   | X | X | X |
| X | X |   | X |
|   |   |   | X |
| X | X |   | X |
| X | X |   | X |
|   | X | X | X |
| X | X |   | X |
| X | X |   | X |
|   | X | X | X |
| X | X |   | X |
|   | X |   | X |
| X |   |   | X |
| X |   | X | X |
| X | X |   | X |
|   |   |   | X |
|   |   | X | X |
| X | X |   | X |
|   | X | X | X |

**Note:** Human Resources will be notified regardless of the Reported Incident category whenever an employee is likely to face any discipline, including possible termination.

# Glossary

**Business Unit** means the internal business organization in which the incident arises. Notification is generally made to the immediate supervisor of the subject of the investigation.

**Senior Manager** means both the senior manager and financial officers in the Home Country. This may include presidents, country managers and zone managers. This may also include the Risk Management and Internal-Audit staffs in the Home Country.

**Home Country** means the country in which the reported incident occurs.

**Legal** means the senior legal advisor in the Home Country.

**Human Resources** means the senior human-resources senior manager in the Home Country.

**Compliance** means the Corporate Compliance department. It may also include an ethics liaison in the Home Country.

**Abuse of Ethics or other Hotline** means an allegation relating to the bad-faith use of the compliance hotline or other reporting processes to harass someone or to file knowingly false information.

**Accounting Irregularities** means an allegation relating to the improper accounting of business transactions, or not following internal accounting and financial-reporting rules. This includes falsifying or forging financial records. This includes the misstatement of expenses, revenues or business transactions. (This does not include branch-level transactions, which are included in "Branch Financial Violations.")

**Branch Financial Violations** means an allegation that someone working in a branch or local office did not follow established procedures for handling financial processes, such as workers-compensation coding, wage/hour issues or handling past-due accounts. This includes the misstatement of branch expenses, branch revenues, or branch-level transactions. (This category does not include an allegation relating to financial reporting that is not on the branch level.)

**Competitive Issues** means an allegation relating to improper sales and marketing practices. This category includes allegations of unfair competition, unethical marketing practices, using a competitor's trade secrets, and making disparaging comments about competitors. An allegation of "unfair competition" includes discussing prices, strategies or sales terms with competitors. It also includes agreements covering customers or territories. This category also includes obtaining information about a competitor in some improper way.

**Conflicts of Interest** means an allegation that someone made a decision while allowing their personal loyalties to conflict or appear to conflict with the company's interests. This category includes hiring or supervising a relative, having a financial, business or personal interest in a company vendor or competitor, or having some outside personal interest that conflicts with the company's interests. This includes outside employment that creates a conflict of interest or diminishes productivity and effectiveness.

**Confidential or Proprietary Information Issues** means an allegation that someone improperly lost, used or possessed non-public information which the company is required to safeguard. This category includes software piracy, improper data copying, and the unauthorized use of someone's patent, copyright and trademark rights. This category includes the improper disclosure of the company business plans, pricing data, marketing programs, personnel information, and financial reports. This category also includes client-related confidential information.

**Customer-site Incident** means an allegation that someone acted improperly at a client location. This category includes on-site illegal activity, theft, vandalism and physical violence. (This category does not apply to misconduct at company premises.)

**Employment Practice Issues** means an allegation that someone acted improperly in the recruiting, hiring, assignment, evaluation, promotion, training, discipline or compensation of an employee. This category includes allegations of discrimination (race, color, gender, national origin, age, marital status, religion, disability, sexual orientation, veteran status or other protected category).

**Fraud** means an allegation that someone deceived the company or someone else for personal gain. This category includes abuse of employee benefits and expense-report fraud. This category includes falsifying or forging business records other than financial records. This category includes embezzlement and mishandling of company funds. (This category does not include an allegation that an associate changed his or her own time card. Falsifying or forging financial records is included in "Accounting Irregularities" or "Branch Financial Violations.")

**Gifts, Gratuities and Entertainment** means an allegation that someone accepted something valuable, such as a gift, tickets or entertainment, from anyone who is trying to influence an the company business decision. The valuable item could be offered by a supplier, customer, supervisor or subordinate, or where the employee solicited the gift, ticket or entertainment. This includes where the gift-giver could seek or receive special favors from the colleague. This also includes entertainment that is not for bona fide business reasons.

**Insider Trading and Securities Violations** means an allegation that someone knew non-public, material, company-related information and then used that information in a stock transaction. "Non-public, material, company-related information" includes financial results, earnings estimates, changes in management, major contract awards and potential acquisitions.

**Internal Business Operation Issues** means an allegation relating to some activity that conflicts with established company business policies, procedures and practices. This category covers allegations that someone did not follow internal manuals, standard business practices or workplace health and safety procedures. (This category does not cover legal, regulatory or accounting violations.)

**Internal Workplace Conduct Issues** means an allegation that someone behaved improperly while on company premises. This category includes harassment, threats, theft of property, offensive speech (not using an internal system), improper employee relationships, and physical violence. This includes improper soliciting and distribution of material. (Allegations relating to discrimination are included in "Employment Practices.")

**International Trade Control Issues** means an allegation relating to improper actions in doing business outside the Home Country. This category includes problems with export licenses, financial transactions, anti-boycott laws, offering or making improper payments to officials outside the Home Country.

**Kickbacks and Bribery** means an allegation that someone made an improper or illegal payment to someone in the Home Country to influence the recipient's business decisions. This category includes offering, paying or accepting a bribe.

**Misuse of Internal Systems** means an allegation that someone improperly used the company's telephone systems, computers, e-mail, voice mail, fax machines, teleconferencing services, copiers, internal data systems, or the Internet. This includes using the systems to send illegal, sexually explicit, abusive, offensive or profane messages. This also includes improperly uploading or downloading information. This also includes using the systems for soliciting funds or distributing information that is unrelated to company business.

**Money Laundering** means an allegation that someone, such as a vendor, tried to "launder" the proceeds of a crime—such as narcotics trafficking, bribery or fraud—in order to hide the money or make the amounts appear legitimate by making it look like a normal business transaction with the company.

**Political and Charitable Activity** issues means an allegation that someone made a payment to a political party, political organization, charity or an elected official that directly affects the company's business interests. This category includes participating in the activities of these organizations. (This category does not include someone's personal political or charitable activities that have no connection to the company.)

**Purchasing Issues** means an allegation relating to buying supplies or services for company use. These allegations relate to how a vendor was chosen, the vendor's qualifications, or the price we were charged for the supplies or services.

**Records and Document Retention Issues** means an allegation that someone did not retain or safeguard company books and records according to the company's document-retention guidelines. This category applies to the retention or destruction of company documents in any form. This category includes destroying or concealing documents in order to avoid retention obligations.

**Regulatory Noncompliance** means an allegation that someone did not follow a government rule or regulation. These rules and regulations include employee-verification requirements, visa and immigration rules, payroll and tax obligations, wage / hour laws, labor-law violations, stock-exchange and other government rules. (This category does not apply to failures to follow internal business procedures because those procedures are not required by the government. This category also does not include falsifying or forging financial records, and those are included in "Accounting Irregularities" or "Branch Financial Violations.")

**Requests for Advice or Clarification** means a request by someone for help understanding an ethics or compliance rule under the Code of Business Conduct before that person takes any action.

**Requests for Assistance** means a request by someone for help resolving an issue that would usually be handled by Human Resources or another business group, but was reported to Compliance. (For example, this category would include a request from a colleague for assistance to resolve a payroll issue.) This category would not involve an issue that falls within the Code of Business Conduct.

**Retaliation of Whistleblowers** means the allegation that someone who reported a possible ethics or compliance-related violation was treated unfairly because he made the report.

**Substance Abuse** means an allegation that someone misused alcohol or drugs (legal or illegal) while at work. This category includes someone using prescription medication if that medication impaired that person's ability to do his or her job properly.

# APPENDIX E

## Notification of Investigation for other Key Internal Departments

**Memo**  **Highly Confidential**

**To:** Steve Smith
**From:**
**Date:** January 1, 2013
**Subject:** New Internal Investigation – Case #000
Chicago, Illinois

---

I write to inform you that an issue for workplace investigation has been brought to our attention. Based on the preliminary information we have, the allegation concerns improper workplace conduct at the _____ branch.

Under our Management Notification Matrix, I am notifying you of this new pending investigation because the nature of the allegation impacts some of your department's responsibilities. I will be contacting employees in this office and in other departments in order to gather the necessary facts and determine whether this allegation can be substantiated. The scope of the investigation or the particular investigation subjects may change as the investigation progresses.

Please know that, regardless of the allegation, no one is presumed to have acted improperly, unethically or in violation of company rules unless the investigation proves otherwise. No conclusions will be made until all the facts have been reviewed.

If you choose, you may participate in the investigation process with me. Additionally, I may call upon you for specific information and/or to obtain relevant documents. I will make sure to update you as the investigation proceeds. As always, please maintain the confidentiality of this allegation and the subsequent investigation.

Please feel free to contact me at (___) ___-_____ with any questions.

# APPENDIX F

## Colleague Referral Guidelines

As part of the company's commitment to an ethical workplace and to ensure that the company meets its legal obligations, the company encourages colleagues and associates, subject to local restrictions and guidelines, to report possible violations of business conduct. The company, through its Corporate Compliance department ("Compliance"), responds to these reports. Compliance also tracks these incidents and reports them to the Board of Directors.

Compliance has primary responsibility to ensure that a detailed investigation of any possible violation has occurred. Compliance, therefore, depends on its colleagues in key internal departments to notify our group when these matters arise. These notifications are essential to allow Compliance to track the incident.

These guidelines are intended only to ensure that Compliance learns that the incident has occurred. These guidelines do not replace a business group's existing procedures for investigating these incidents. However, following the guidelines will allow our group to collaborate in investigations when it is appropriate for us to do so.

You will be expected to investigate an allegation of misconduct if it meets each of these requirements:

1. The report is made by an associate, colleague or third-party acting in good faith who genuinely believes that misconduct may have occurred.
2. The report relates to possible associate or colleague misconduct, and the report does not solely relate to a personnel-management issue.
3. On the face of the facts given by the reporter, the manager believes that misconduct may have occurred.
4. It is determined that the relevant facts of the suspected misconduct—regardless of how the reporter characterizes them—fall within one of these incident categories.

Please contact Compliance if you learn of an allegation that an associate, colleague or franchisee may have been involved in any of these:

**Accounting Irregularities:** the improper accounting of business transaction, or not following internal accounting and financial-reporting rules. This includes falsifying or forging financial records, or misstating expenses, revenues or business transactions.

**Branch Financial Violations:** someone working in a branch or local office did not follow established financial procedures for handling financial processes, such as workers-compensation coding, wage/hour issues or handling past-due accounts.

**Competitive Issues:** improper sales and marketing practices such as unfair competition, unethical marketing practices, and making disparaging comments about competitors. An allegation of "unfair competition" includes discussing prices, strategies or sales terms with competitors. It also includes agreements covering customers or territories. This category also includes obtaining competitor information in some improper way.

**Conflicts of Interest:** someone made a business decision while allowing their personal loyalties to conflict or appear to conflict with the company's interests. This includes hiring or supervising a relative, having a business or personal interest in a company vendor or competitor, or having some outside personal interest that conflicts with the company's interests. This also includes outside employment that creates a conflict of interest.

**Confidential or Proprietary Information Issues:** someone improperly lost, used or possessed information which the company is required to safeguard. This includes software piracy, improper data copying, and unauthorized use of someone's copyright or trademark rights. This also includes the improper disclosure of the company business plans, pricing data, marketing programs, personnel information, financial reports, and client-related information.

**Customer-site Incident:** someone acted improperly at a client location. This includes on-site illegal activity, theft, vandalism and physical violence.

**Employment Practice Issues:** someone acted improperly in the recruiting, hiring, evaluation, promotion, training, discipline or compensation of an employee. This includes discrimination (race, color, gender, national origin, age, marital status, religion, disability, sexual orientation, veteran status or other protected category).

**Fraud:** someone deceived the company or someone else for personal gain. This includes abuse of employee benefits and expense-report fraud. This includes falsifying business records, as well as embezzlement or mishandling of company funds.

**Gifts, Gratuities and Entertainment:** someone accepted something valuable, such as a gift, tickets or entertainment, from anyone trying to influence a company business decision. The valuable item could be offered by a supplier, customer, supervisor or subordinate, or if the employee solicited the gift, ticket or entertainment. This also includes entertainment that is not for bona fide business reasons.

**Insider Trading and Securities Violations:** someone knew non-public, material, company-related information and then used that information in a stock transaction. "Non-public, material, company-related information" includes financial results, earnings estimates, changes in executive management, major contract awards and potential acquisitions.

**Internal Business Operation Issues:** some business activity that violates established company business policies, procedures and practices. This includes allegations that someone intentionally did not follow internal manuals, standard business practices, or workplace health and safety procedures.

**Internal Workplace Conduct Issues:** someone behaved improperly while on company premises. This includes harassment, threats, theft of property, offensive speech (not using an internal system), improper employee relationships, and physical violence. This includes improper soliciting and distribution of material.

**International Trade Control Issues:** someone acted improperly in order to do company business in another country. This includes problems with export licenses, financial transactions, anti-boycott laws, offering or making improper payments to officials in the other country.

**Kickbacks and Bribery:** someone made an improper or illegal payment to someone for company business that is intended to influence the recipient's business decisions. This includes offering, paying or accepting a bribe.

**Misuse of Internal Systems:** someone improperly used the company's telephone systems, voice mail, fax machines, computers, e-mail, teleconferencing services, copiers, internal data systems, or the Internet. This includes using the systems to send illegal, sexually explicit, abusive, offensive or profane messages. This also includes improperly uploading or downloading information. This also includes using company systems for soliciting funds or distributing information that is unrelated to company business.

**Money Laundering:** someone, such as a vendor, tried to "launder" the proceeds of a crime—such as narcotics trafficking, bribery or fraud—in order to hide the money or make the amounts appear legitimate by making it look like a normal business transaction with the company.

**Political and Charitable Activity Issues:** someone made a payment to a political party, charity, political organization or an elected official that directly affects the company's business interests. This includes participating in the activities of that organization. (This does not apply to someone's personal political or charitable activities that have no effect on the company's business.)

**Purchasing Issues:** someone acted improperly when buying supplies or services for company use. The allegation relates to how a vendor was chosen, the vendor's qualifications, or the price we were charged for the supplies or services.

**Records and Document Retention Issues:** someone did not retain or safeguard company books and records according to the company's document-retention guidelines. This applies to the retention or destruction of company documents. This includes destroying or concealing documents in order to avoid retention requirements.

**Regulatory Noncompliance:** someone did not follow a government rule or regulation. These rules and regulations include employee-verification requirements, visa and immigration rules, payroll and tax obligations, wage / hour laws, labor-law violations, stock-exchange and other government rules.

**Retaliation of Whistleblowers:** someone who reported a possible ethics or compliance-related violation was treated unfairly because he made the report.

**Substance Abuse:** someone misused alcohol or drugs (legal or illegal) while at work. This includes someone using prescription medication if that medication impaired that person's ability to do his or her job properly.

# APPENDIX G

## Guidelines for Outside Counsel

**Memo**

**To:** Outside Counsel
**From:**
**Date:** January 1, 2013
**Subject:** Guidelines for Misconduct Investigations

---

The Corporate Compliance department ("Compliance") implements and oversees legal-compliance and comprehensive business-ethics programs throughout the company. The Code of Conduct applies to all temporary and full-time employees. From time to time, circumstances arise within the conduct of the company's business that leads to allegations of misconduct by an employee of the company, or a potential violation of law or regulation.

### *Referrals*

It is the company's policy to investigate thoroughly all allegations of legal or ethical misconduct, whether committed by full-time employees or temporary employees. The investigation process is conducted in a manner that treats those affected with dignity and fairness.

When Compliance learns of an allegation of possible legal or ethical misconduct, we review the matter to determine whether an investigation is required. If so, we will open an investigation of the matter. In many instances, we conduct the investigation in-house, without the assistance of outside counsel. We conduct the investigation according to our specified investigation protocol, which applies to all company investigations.

Under certain circumstances, it is appropriate to have the matter investigated by outside counsel. Regardless of whether the investigation is conduct internally or by outside counsel, however, each investigation should follow the same standards to ensure the confidentiality, objectivity and impartiality of the investigation. This will help to ensure that the investigation is adequately documented if the company must later defend how the investigation was conducted.

Your investigation should, to the extent possible, preserve the company's attorney-client privilege. Your findings should make clear that the investigation is for the purpose of providing legal advice to the company and, if appropriate under the circumstances, is being conducted in anticipation of litigation.

When we refer a matter to outside counsel for investigation, we will define for you the scope of that investigation based on the information available at that time. Generally, the scope of the investigation will be to determine (i) whether the particular allegation(s) can be substantiated by the facts elicited during the investigation, and (ii) to identify relevant areas for the improvement of the operations, efficiency or effectiveness of the department involved. (For example, an investigation may find that there is ineffective management supervision, insufficient training or the lack of a needed corporate policy.) Your investigation should not be conducted simply to uncover sufficient facts to determine if misconduct occurred.

The company uses the findings of its workplace investigations to improve our business, either by identifying areas of unacceptable business risk or flawed business operations, which expose the company needlessly. The business goals of the investigation include any of the following:

- Minimizing business risk;
- Identifying weaknesses in business operations;
- Removing certain individuals from the company;
- Recovering company assets that were lost because of the misconduct;
- Obtaining the criminal prosecution of those involved;
- Protecting the company's public image and reputation;
- Preparing for anticipated civil or criminal litigation involving the company.

Information developed from an investigation maximizes options for those managers who must decide on the solution. We partner with our management to identify and quantify risks to our business.

The company's standard investigation protocol is specified in the "Guide to Conducting Internal Business Investigations." This protocol should be followed unless you determine that some valid reason exists to deviate from it. A copy of the guide is attached to this memorandum.

## Interviews and Documents

Investigations will often involve interviewing the company employees and those temporary employees assigned to work for the company's customers. The person being interviewed should be treated with dignity and fairness. The integrity of our workplace investigation process and the perception among employees that the process is fair is critically important to our business goals.

At the beginning of the interview, the interviewer should describe in general terms the nature and purpose of the interview. The interviewer should also read our "Instructions for Witnesses" document to the witness. A copy of the document is attached to this memorandum.

Please invite the witness to submit a written personal statement of the relevant facts if the witness wishes to do so. Please ensure that the statement is signed and dated. The statement should be added to the investigation file. A template document is attached to this memorandum for your use.

Please draft an interview memorandum shortly after the interview. This memorandum should specify exactly what happened in the interview, including direct quotes and any admissions. Once the memorandum has been drafted, any handwritten notes or other documentation about the interview should be destroyed so that there is only one statement of what transpired at the interview. You may retain the memorandum in your investigation file unless you believe it is important to share that information with us earlier.

We will assist you to obtain any company documents you believe are relevant to the investigation. We may also designate other company contacts, such as a member of Human Resources, to assist you.

## Written Report

Once you have completed your fact finding, please prepare a written report of the results of the investigation. You may also offer recommendations about proposed corrective action. A template document is attached to this memorandum for your use.

We use written reports to assist management to develop corrective procedures to avoid repetitions of questionable conduct. We also use the reports, where necessary, to communicate to third parties that wrongful conduct did not occur or that corrective action has been taken internally.

Please do not offer any recommendations about possible disciplinary action against specific employees because this is outside the scope of the investigation. To ensure consistent administration of sanctions across the company, disciplinary action is handled internally by our Human Resources department and the relevant business group management. Similarly, please do not offer any recommendations regarding whether the company should compensate someone.

In order to preserve the attorney-client privilege, the report should be marked confidential, and the report should be distributed only to us.

## *Possible Problems*

During the course of your investigation, certain problems may arise. We address some of them here to recommend how they should be handled on our behalf.

The company policy and applicable law protect whistleblowers and similar persons against retaliation for reporting incidents of possible or actual misconduct. It is absolutely prohibited for any person who participates in a company investigation to be penalized in any manner because of their participation. Please contact us immediately if you have reason to believe that any form of retaliation may have occurred or may be threatened.

You may not compel any person to submit to an interview during the investigation. As an employer, the company may have certain recourse against such an employee for their refusal to submit to the interview. Therefore, if an employee refuses, please inform the employee that you will not force the employee to be interviewed, and that you will refer the issue to us to address the matter with the witness's superiors. Please contact us as soon as possible after the meeting.

During the course of an interview, your fact-finding may uncover additional facts that may indicate that additional violations or more-serious misconduct has occurred. Similarly, you may believe that your investigation should be expanded to include additional investigation subjects. If you uncover such facts, please contact us immediately to discuss the matter. Please do not expand the scope of your investigation without discussing it with us first.

Employees may ask you whether they are in trouble or whether they will be disciplined. Be straightforward—it is certainly possible that employees may be disciplined if they engage in misconduct, but please emphasize that your role in the investigation is to determine the true facts so management may be advised accordingly. Never represent to a witness that the company may consider their cooperation to be a quid pro quo for avoiding any disciplinary, civil or criminal action.

A witness may ask if he needs the assistance of a lawyer. This poses a problem that requires an immediate response. While everyone has the right to consult an attorney, the company has the right to require its employees to disclose information that is relevant to the company's business. Please offer no opinion on whether the witness needs a lawyer. Please remind the witness that you are representing the company and cannot provide the witness with any legal advice. (Your notes should state the substance of this exchange during the interview.) The company is not required to allow interview subjects to have a lawyer present and can insist that the interview continue with the witness without a lawyer present. If this situation arises, please contact us to discuss further steps.

An employee may ask if she may have a co-worker present during the interview. We generally accommodate these requests if (i) the co-worker has no connection to the matter under investigation, and (ii) the co-worker does not interfere with the questioning or the answers offered by the witness. However, you may, at your discretion, decline the request if you believe that it would negatively impact the interview.

At the beginning of an investigation and at various points during its course, you should make a good-faith assessment whether the matter under investigation poses the risk of criminal liability for the company or any of the employees. If so, inform the witness of the option to retain personal counsel and have the personal counsel present during the interview. If requested, be prepared to postpone or suspend the interview long enough to permit the witness to obtain counsel or consider whether to do so.

Please contact us immediately if you believe that, for some reason, the company should take some interim action pending the completion of the investigation, such as the suspension of an employee or the seizure of documents and equipment. The company will take whatever steps are reasonably necessary to protect the safety of our employees and to protect the integrity of the company's policies and procedures.

If you believe during the investigation, that any criminal activity may have occurred, please contact us immediately. Unless there is some immediate risk, do not contact any law-enforcement agency without our prior consent and participation.

# APPENDIX H

## Management Notification of Investigation

**Memo**

**To:** Steve Smith
**From:**
**Date:** January 1, 2013
**Subject:** New Internal Investigation – Case #000
Chicago, Illinois

---

I write to inform you that an issue for workplace investigation has been brought to our attention. Based on the preliminary information we have, the allegation concerns improper workplace conduct by _____, a member of the branch staff.

I am notifying you of this new pending investigation because the allegation pertains to an office within your territory. I will be contacting employees in this office and in other departments in order to gather the necessary facts and determine whether this allegation can be substantiated. The scope of the investigation or the particular investigation subjects may change as the investigation progresses.

Please know that, regardless of the allegation, no one is presumed to have acted improperly, unethically or in violation of company rules unless the investigation proves otherwise. No conclusions will be made until all the facts have been reviewed.

You may be called upon to assist me in conducting the investigation by facilitating certain interviews and/or obtaining relevant documents. I will make sure to update you as the investigation proceeds. As always, please maintain the confidentiality of this allegation and the subsequent investigation.

Please feel free to contact me at (___) ___-____ with any questions.

# APPENDIX I

## Request for Interview

**Memo**

**To:** Steve Smith
**From:**
**Date:** January 1, 2013
**Subject:** Internal Investigation – Case #000
Chicago, Illinois

---

I write to confirm our telephone conversation. As I told you, an allegation has been raised that we would like to discuss with you. We have already gathered some preliminary information regarding the situation, and we would like to speak to you because we believe you have information that is relevant to the matters under investigation. I cannot share details concerning the matter today and ask you not to discuss our conversation with anyone in the company.

I would like to meet with you as soon as possible. Would you be available to meet with me in your office at 9:00 on January 9th?

The purpose of this meeting is to gather information regarding the issue and your role in the situation. I will be asking you specific questions regarding your recollections and observations. I will also ask you for any documents you have that may be relevant to the investigation.

Your honesty, truthfulness, and confidentiality are critical to resolve this situation as soon as possible. Please know that, regardless of the allegation, no one is presumed to have acted improperly, unethically or in violation of company rules unless the investigation proves otherwise. No conclusions will be made until all the facts have been reviewed.

Please feel free to contact me at (___) ___-____ with any questions.

# APPENDIX J

## Request for Subject Interview

**Memo**

**To:** Steve Smith
**From:**
**Date:** January 1, 2013
**Subject:** Internal Investigation – Case #000
Chicago, Illinois

---

I write to confirm our telephone conversation. As I told you, an allegation has been raised that we would like to discuss with you. We have already gathered some preliminary information regarding the situation, and we would like to speak to you because we believe you have information that is relevant to the matters under investigation. Please know that the allegation involves you personally.

I would like to meet with you as soon as possible. Would you be available to meet with me in your office at 9:00 on January 9th?

The purpose of this meeting is to gather information regarding the issue and your role in the situation. I will be asking you specific questions regarding your recollections and observations. I will also ask you for any documents you have that may be relevant to the investigation.

Because the allegation involves you personally, we want to give you the opportunity to confirm or deny certain of the facts we have uncovered. We also want to allow you to give us your account of these events. This interview may be your best opportunity to explain your role in the matters under review.

Your honesty, truthfulness, and confidentiality are critical to resolve this situation as soon as possible. Please know that, regardless of the allegation, no one is presumed to have acted improperly, unethically or in violation of company rules unless the investigation proves otherwise. No conclusions will be made until all the facts have been reviewed.

Please feel free to contact me at (___) ___-____ with any questions.

# APPENDIX K

## Instructions to Witnesses

This is a workplace investigation. It is a serious matter. You have been asked to assist us. We are trying to find out what happened here so we can advise management accordingly. We appreciate your time and cooperation.

I will not mislead you or lie to you. You should not lie to me. Lying in the course of the investigation can get you in serious trouble.

If you are an attorney, add: Please know that I am a lawyer. I represent the company, and I do not represent you. Anything we discuss here today is not subject to the attorney-client privilege, and I may share this information with company management.

You should cooperate fully, with complete candor, and respond to all questions and requests honestly. If you do not understand a question, please let me know, and I will clarify it. If you do not ask for a clarification, I will assume you understood the question.

I am interested in what you know based on your own personal knowledge. Please do not speculate. If you do not know the answer to a question, please say so. Don't guess.

We presume that anyone suspected of acting illegally, unethically, or in violation of company policy is innocent until the investigation proves otherwise. We will make no conclusions until all the facts have been reviewed.

Investigations are conducted confidentially. Do not discuss this investigation with anyone, unless I tell you otherwise. Information is disclosed internally only on a need-to-know basis.

We will not tolerate any type of threat or retaliation against anyone who reports a violation or cooperates in an investigation. If you receive any such threats, please advise me immediately. I will give you my business card.

Do not ask me who reported a violation or who else may be cooperating in the investigation. We want to protect the reputation of anyone involved in the investigation, and you do not necessarily know the full scope of our inquiries.

Do not play detective. Do not draw any conclusions as a result of this interview. This interview is only part of the investigation.

Please keep all records relating to the investigation. Don't destroy anything.

My goal is to obtain the best information possible. If you later remember anything that you couldn't remember here today, or you want to supplement or correct something you said, please call me. I would be happy to make the necessary changes.

If you want, you may give me a written statement concerning the matters we are discussing. This is entirely voluntary. You have no obligation to do so. However, this will give you the chance to explain the facts as you believe them to be. I have the form for your use if you choose to make such a statement. I will then add it to the investigations file.

# APPENDIX L

## Personal Statement

**Your Details:**
**Name:**
**Title:**
**Office Location:**
**Phone:**

___

Your statement (attach additional sheets to this page if needed):




**This statement is true to the best of my knowledge and belief. I understand that I will be subject to company discipline if I have willfully stated anything that I know to be false or do not believe to be true.**

Signed: _____  Date: _____

# APPENDIX M

## Final Investigation Report

**Case Number:**
**Business Unit:**
**Location:**
**Investigator:**
**Report Date:**

This final report is prepared in connection with the investigation. The report is based on supporting documents provided in the course of the investigation, an understanding of the relevant facts and on information collected during the course of the investigation.

The investigation has been limited solely to a determination of the relevant facts. No opinion is offered regarding the findings, possible disciplinary decisions, or considerations of potential legal liability.

1. *Investigation location*
   The company business group is _____. The company office is located at _____.

2. *The report*
   The misconduct allegations investigated were:
   The investigation determined that the allegations of misconduct are: (substantiated or unsubstantiated).

3. *Investigative steps*
   The investigation sought to establish whether the allegations could be proven by the available facts and, regardless of the outcome, the various policy and process improvements that could be improved.
   Interviews were taken as part of the investigation. Interviews were taken of each of the following employees:

The key documents reviewed were:

4. *Findings on the allegation*
**Summary of findings:** The allegation was (substantiated or unsubstantiated). Specifically:

**Specific factual findings:**

5. *Post-investigation information*

6. *Evaluation of business processes and internal controls*

# APPENDIX N

## No Retaliation Memorandum

**Memo**

**To:** Department Employees
**From:**
**Date:** January 1, 2013
**Subject:** Reminder of Policy against Retaliation

---

As you know, we recently concluded an investigation involving one or more people in your department. Out of an abundance of caution, we wanted to remind each of you that the company prohibits you from retaliating against anyone who lodged a complaint against a co-worker—whether it has merit or not—or cooperated with the investigation.

It is human nature for a person who was the subject of an investigation or who had to submit to an interview to have hard feelings or believe that others may have been causing problems for the company. When people begin to act on those feelings in a negative way, they may be engaging in conduct that could be viewed as retaliation.

Although there is no complete list, acts of retaliation include each of the following:

- Discussing or gossiping about the report or a witness's participation in the investigation;
- Openly laughing at or referring to the employee in a harsh or derogatory way;
- Ignoring or avoiding the employee in an obvious manner;
- Failing to provide the employee with critical information needed to perform his job or ensure his personal safety in the workplace;
- Blaming the employee for causing a problem because the employee filed a complaint;
- Remarking that the employee should transfer to another department or quit his job;
- Threatening or harassing the employee.

Because the investigation is complete, the company now considers the matter closed. The company will take whatever actions, if any, that it deems appropriate. There is no valid business reason for continuing to address these matters, and we appreciate your cooperation as we move forward.

# APPENDIX O

## Business Ethics Bulletin

As part of our commitment to an ethical workplace and to ensure that the company meets its legal obligations, the company requires colleagues and associates to report possible violations of the Code of Business Conduct. The company responds to these reports. From time to time, the lessons learned from an investigation are relevant to the operations of other business groups. We would like to inform you about the results of a recent investigation which may be of interest to you.

**Incident**

After a routine audit, a client alleged that they were fraudulently overbilled for services. Compliance investigated the matter and determined that the company on-site supervisor (the "Supervisor") at the client's location falsified timecards and then kept the over-payment. The Supervisor refused to cooperate with the investigation and was terminated. Law-enforcement managers were also contacted.

The Supervisor had near-total management control over the associates at the site. The branch's internal processes allowed the Supervisor—without the involvement of anyone else—to (i) enter "open orders" in the system; (ii) assign an associate to fill that order; (iii) handle the time cards; (iv) calculate the invoice and instruct the branch to send the invoice to the client; (v) have associate checks delivered to the branch; and (vi) retrieve those checks from the branch office and distribute them to the associates.

When an associate's assignment was temporarily suspended, however, the order was not closed as it should have been. Instead, the Supervisor falsified timecards for that idled associate to make it appear as if the associate had actually worked that week.

When weekly payroll checks were generated for the associates, the check would be directed to the branch if that associate had not arranged for direct deposit. The normal practice was for the Supervisor to retrieve the checks from the branch and distribute them to the associates. Of course, if an associate did not work that week and the timecard was fabricated, the Supervisor took the check, cashed it at a check-cashing service that participated in the scheme, and kept the money. (Because the associate did not work that week, that associate would not have expected a check.)

**Key Takeaways**

**Cause of Incident:** Procedures placed too much authority solely with the Supervisor. The failure to close "open orders" when an associate would be temporarily idle created the opportunity for the fraud. This was compounded by allowing the Supervisor to handle timecards, obtain associate paychecks and distribute these checks without the participation of others. The fraud would likely not have happened if another colleague had been involved in the process.

Branch managers who are responsible for on-site supervisors should examine their own procedures to ensure that sufficient controls are in place to prevent such a fraud from occurring.

**Policy Violated:** The Code of Conduct states that: "All employees are required to understand and abide by internal financial control procedures relating to their job functions [including]. . . .complete and accurate entries on time sheets and expense reports" and "accurate record keeping."

Falsification of billing records and fraud is serious misconduct and a business-ethics violation that will result in severe disciplinary action, up to and including termination.

The monetary value related to an ethics violation does not mitigate the severity of the offense or the resulting disciplinary action.

**Escalation Process:** Any colleague or associate should immediately report any suspected ethics or compliance-related violation to his Supervisor or Employee Relations, or call the Ethics hotline. The hotline accepts anonymous calls. the company policy forbids retaliation against any employee who comes forward with a good-faith complaint of inappropriate conduct.

**Additional Resources:** The Code of Conduct is available externally at _____. For further training and guidance on business conduct and ethics, visit www._____.com.

Release Date:

Contact for Additional Information:

# APPENDIX P

## Close-out with Reporter

**Memo**

**To:**       Steve Smith
**From:**
**Date:**     January 1, 2013
**Subject:**  Internal Investigation – Case #000
              Thank You and Follow Up

---

We write regarding the information you recently provided to the company regarding a possible violation of ethics rules or company procedures. This note is to inform you that we have just recently completed our workplace investigation.

We appreciate your cooperation during this process. Your involvement has been important to the company's commitment to maintaining the highest standards of ethical conduct and business integrity.

Although the details of our investigation are confidential, the findings have been shared with the relevant members of management. If appropriate, corrective steps will be taken to address the matter.

Please feel free to contact me at (___) ___-____ with any questions. Thank you again for your assistance.

# SOURCES

American Institute of Certified Public Accountants. *The CPA's Handbook of Fraud and Commercial Crime Prevention*. Durham, NC: American Institute of Certified Public Accountants 2003.

ASIS International. *Investigations Management*. Alexandria, VA: ASIS International, 2006.

Association of Certified Fraud Examiners. *2006 Fraud Examiners Manual*. Austin, TX: Association of Certified Fraud Examiners, 2006.

Association of Certified Fraud Examiners. *2006 Report to the Nation on Occupational Fraud and Abuse*. Austin, TX: Association of Certified Fraud Examiners, 2006.

Association of Certified Fraud Examiners. *Conducting Compliance Investigations*. Austin, TX: Association of Certified Fraud Examiners, 2003.

Association of Corporate Counsel. *Corporate Compliance*. Washington, DC: Association of Corporate Counsel, October 2004.

Association of Corporate Counsel. *The Ethical Minefield for In House Counsel*. Washington, DC: Association of Corporate Counsel, 2003.

Babitsky, Steven and James J. Mangraviti. *Writing and Defending your Expert Report*. Falmouth, MA: Seak, 2002.

Bologna, Jack and Paul Shaw. *Corporate Crime Investigation*. Amsterdam: Elsevier, Butterworth-Heinemann, 1997.

Booden, Michael R. *Conducting Effective Internal Investigations*. Washington, DC: Association of Corporate Counsel, 2004.

Bratton, Eleanor and Daniel Long. *Compliance Investigations: Avoiding Common Mistakes*. Albuquerque: Modrall Sperling, 1995.

Brennan, James and Jeffrey Kaplan. "Making Compliance Training Effective." *GC New York* (July 25, 2005).

Brian, Brad and Barry McNeil. *Compliance Corporate Investigations*. Chicago: American Bar Association, 2003.

Cole, Richard. *Management of Compliance Business Investigations: A Survival Guide*. Springfield, IL: Charles Thomas, 1996.

CEB Compliance and Ethics Leadership Council. *Council Toolkit: Conducting Internal Investigations*. Washington, DC: CEB Compliance and Ethics Leadership Council, 2004.

CEB Compliance and Ethics Leadership Council. *Safeguarding the Corporation*, Washington, DC: CEB Compliance and Ethics Leadership Council, 2006.

CEB Legal Leadership Council. *Employing Legal Privilege to Protect Compliance Audits and Risk Assessments*. Washington, DC: CEB Legal Leadership Council, 2005.

Dempsey, Steve S. *Introduction to Investigations*. Belmont, CA: Thomson Wadsworth, 2003.

Duggan, Sarah Helene. "Compliance Corporate Investigations: Legal Ethics, Professionalism and the Employee Interview." *Columbia Business Law Review*, 859 (2003).

Edwards, Deborah L., Mark Colloway and Brian Edwards. *What to Do When the Whistle Blows: Do's and Don'ts of Compliance Investigations*. Washington, DC: Association of Corporate Counsel, 2004.

Ferraro, Eugene F. *Investigations in the Workplace*. Boca Raton, FL: Auerbach Publications, 2006.

Haig, Robert. *Successful Partnering between Inside and Outside Counsel*. Eagan, MN: Thomson West, 2004.

Hancock, William (ed.). *Corporate Counsel's Guide to Legal Audits and Investigations*. Chesterland, OH: Business Laws, Inc., 2005.

Harrison, Orrin. "Conducting Corporate Investigations under the Increased Scrutiny of Sarbanes-Oxley." *Securities Regulation Law Journal*, (Fall, Hasl-

Kelchner, Hanna. *The Business Guide to Legal Literacy*. San Francisco: Jossey-Bass, 2006.

Hogge, Raymond L. "How to Conduct a Lawful Workplace Investigation." *Virginia Labor Law* (June 1998).

Johnson, William C. and Williams, Neal O. *Liar, Liar, Pants on Fire: How to Establish an Effective Compliance Investigations Program*. Paper presented at the 2002 Association of Corporate Counsel annual meeting.

Kahn Consulting, Inc., *How to Conduct a Corporate Internal Investigations; Reference Materials.* Washington, DC: Association of Corporate Counsel, 2004.

Koletar, Joseph W. *Fraud Exposed.* New York: John Wiley & Sons, 2003.

Kuehne, Benedict. "Protecting the Privilege in the Corporate Setting: Conducting and Defending Compliance Corporate Investigations." *St. Thomas Law Review.* 9:651 (1997).

*Managing the Risk of Fraud: A Guide for Managers.* London: Her Majesty's Treasury, May 2003.

Marmer, Ronald L., Stauffer, Robert R., Schrantz, Erin R., and Moran, Molly J. "How to Conduct Internal Corporate Investigations after Sarbanes-Oxley." *ALI-ABA Business Law Course Materials Journal.* (December 2004..

McMahon, Rory J. *Practical Handbook for Professional Investigators.* Boca Raton, FL:CRC Press, 2007.

Muller, Deborah. "As the Table Turns: How to Maintain the Upper Hand When Conducting a Workplace Investigation." *Workforce Management Online* (November 2007).

Pfadenhauer, Diane M. "Workplace Investigations: Rethinking the Traditional Paradigm and Advocating the Use of Third-Party Investigators." *HR Advisor* (July 2005).

Propper, Eugene. *Corporate Fraud Investigations and Compliance Programs.* Dobbs Ferry, NY: Oceana Publications, 2000.

Rabon, Don. *Interviewing and Interrogation.* Durham, NC: Carolina Academic Press, 1992.

Rabon, Don. *Investigative Discourse Analysis.* Durham, NC: Carolina Academic Press, 2003.

Richards, Dave. "Envisioning our Future." *Internal Auditor* (August 2001).

Schiff, Matthew B. and Kramer, Linda C. "Conducting Internal Investigations of Employee Theft and Other Misconduct." *The Brief* (Spring 2004).

Sennewald, Charles A. and Tsukayama, Steve. *The Process of Investigation: Concepts and Strategies for Investigators in the Private Sector.* Amsterdam: Elsevier, 2006.

Shenk, Maury D. and Schneck, Melanie. "Should a Corporation Report a Breach to Law Enforcement." *Secure Business Quarterly* (3rd Qtr. 2001).

Silverstein, Ira. "Hear No Evil, See No Evil No Longer Viable." *Outside Counsel* (2005).

Steinberg, Marc I. *Attorney Liability after Sarbanes-Oxley.* New York: Law Journal Press, 2005.

Taylor, David F. "What if It's an Inside Job." *Business Law Today* (September/October 2005).

Thompson, Steve. "How to Conduct an Effective Investigation." *CIO* (June 6, 2007).

Turner, Jonathan. "Steps to Take When Referring your Case for Prosecution." *Preventing Business Fraud* (March 2002).

Webb, Dan K. *Corporate Compliance Investigations.* New York: Law Journal Press, 2004.

Welch, Jack. *Winning.* New York: HarperBusiness, 2005.

Wells, Joseph. "Let Them Know Someone's Watching." *Journal of Accountancy* (May 2002).

Wells, Joseph. "New Approaches to Fraud Deterrence." *Journal of Accountancy* (Feb. 2004).

Wells, Joseph. "Why Employees Commit Fraud." *Journal of Accountancy* (Feb. 2001).

Yeschke, Charles. *The Art of Investigative Interviewing.* Amsterdam: Elsevier, Butterworth Heinemann, 2003.